You Can Win With Love

You Can Win With Love

by

Dale E. Galloway

HARVEST HOUSE PUBLISHERS
IRVINE, CALIFORNIA 92714

Foreword

Someone once said, "Write the truth but never write about an *unlearned* truth."

You Can Win With Love is a book about a *learned* truth. Dale Galloway has climbed from the deep valleys of self-loathing and loneliness to the dizzying heights of acceptance and love. His journey has shaped him into a rare and sensitive man.

When he writes chapters entitled
   "Without Love I am Beaten"
   "Whoever Said It Was Easy To Love?"
   "Love Begins At Home"
or he asks,
   "Can Love Be Repaired?"
he is speaking truthfully from the shoulder and the heart. He has LIVED and experienced these pages and God's unmistakable authority can be "clearly" seen and felt.

For me, he summed up this book by writing,
   "The name of the Christian game is—to receive God's choice love gift and become a Christian— then grow in love into everything that name means."

There it is—the learned truth. Read this book for two reasons: to learn and to enjoy!

Joyce Landorf

Contents

I dedicate this book to my children:

Brian Scott

Lynette Kaye

Ann Margaret

who have added so many

new and wonderful dimensions to my love.

CHAPTER 1

Without Love I Am Beaten

Beginning right now, and in the pages to come, I am going to share with you the tremendous truth about GOD'S KIND OF LOVE . . . THAT IS:

TOUCHING ME

LIFTING ME

CHALLENGING ME

WARMING ME

CHANGING ME

WHAT OUR WORLD NEEDS—NOW—IS LOVE!

The phone rang in the home of high society Boston. On the other end of the line was a son who had just returned from Viet Nam and was calling from California. His folks were the pseudo-cocktail circuit, wife-swapping party kind. The boy said to his mother, "I just called, Mother, to tell you that I wanted to bring a buddy home with me." His mother said, "Sure, bring him along for a few days." "But, Mother, there is something that you need to know about this boy. One leg is gone, one arm's gone, one eye's gone, and his face is quite disfigured. Is it all right if I bring him home?"

His mother said, "Bring him home for just a few days." The son said, "You didn't understand me, Mother. I want to bring him home to live with us." The mother began to make all kinds of excuses about embarrassment and what people would think . . . and the phone clicked.

A few hours later the police called from California to Boston. The mother picked up the phone again. The police sergeant at the other end said, "We just found a boy with one arm, one leg, one eye, and a mangled face, who has just killed himself with a shot in the head. The identification papers on the body say he is your son.[1] Without love, what do we have? Nothing—but one ugly scene after another.

As the second hand on the clock moves, so we all live in a world filled with:
Fighting
Hurting
Broken
Lonely
Perishing
    People.

1. Dale E. Galloway, *Dream A New Dream* (Wheaton, Illinois: Tyndale Publishers, 1975) page 73-74.

Estrangement and alienation characterize twentieth century men. The world war of hate and violence never stops—it goes on day and night. The problem of what psychologists call human relationships is staggering. Man's inability to get along with his fellow man is a constant threat to the structure of our civilization. MAN DESPERATELY NEEDS HELP!

THE BIBLE TELLS US—THAT GOD'S KIND OF LOVE—IS THE MEDICINE FOR THE SICKNESS OF OUR WORLD.

APART FROM THE GOD OF LOVE, WE CHRISTIAN'S KNOW THERE IS NO SOLUTION TO MAN'S GREATEST PROBLEM. Many of the finest minds in America, when they are honest, must admit they are at wits end when it comes to helping people get along with one another.

Although we have more counselors, more teachers, more social workers, and more psychiatrists than ever before, we are losing ground. Man's problems are overwhelming us all because of the lack of love. Without love, man perishes from a variety of diseases of mind and body. When love is missing—hate, greed, contempt, and open hostility take over.

Even before we are born, we need to be loved. From experiments conducted in prenatal care, medical experts are now telling us that even an unborn fetus needs to feel the healthy vibrations of love. An unloving atmosphere during pregnancy may do harm to a child's later emotional development. After the baby is born, it needs to be surrounded with an atmosphere of love—to be touched, to be held, to be cuddled, and to be spoken to with words of love. Without love, it has been proven a little baby can actually die. We have already loved our little toddler, Ann, into loving us back. When she kisses Daddy and Mommy, it is so much fun! LOVE IS WHAT HELPS US TO REALLY LIVE, AT ALL AGES!

WHO NEEDS LOVE?
    LITTLE GIRLS NEED LOVE
    BOYS NEED LOVE
    TEENAGERS NEED LOVE
    PARENTS NEED LOVE
    GRANDMAS AND GRANDPAS NEED LOVE
    SINGLE PERSONS NEED LOVE
    WE ALL NEED LOVE
        ESPECIALLY ME,
          I NEED LOVE!
            HOW ABOUT YOU??

MAN'S HEART HAS AN UNQUENCHABLE
THIRST FOR LOVE
NOTHING ELSE SATISFIES
TO BE LOVED IS THE
MOST DESPERATE OF HUMAN NEEDS!

Dr. Thomas P. Malone talked about our greatest need today when he said, "In my practice at the Atlanta Psychiatric Clinic, people sometimes ask me what psychiatry is all about. To me, the answer is increasingly clear. Almost every emotional problem can be summed up in one particular behavior: It's a person walking around screaming, 'For God's sake, love me.' Love me—that is all. He goes through a million different manipulations to get somebody to love him." LET'S FACE IT . . . OUR GREATEST NEED AS HUMAN BEINGS IS TO BE LOVED!

Richard Strauss tells how a dedicated Christian father told him that his ten year old daughter was becoming cold and indifferent toward him. As the father evaluated the situation, he realized that he was cuddling and carrying her younger brother, who was handicapped, but was pushing the daughter aside with comments such as "You're a big girl. You can take care of yourself." However, when the alerted father began to demonstrate openly and enthusiastically his love for her, she blossomed into a very warm and loving little girl, who enjoyed snuggling up to her daddy. [2]

Yes, this old world of ours, torn apart by hatred and strife, where the victim and victims are both lonely and hurt, is crying out of its most desperate human need for the love of God to come to earth through Christ and His children.

Let us clarify the kind of love about which we are talking. You see, people today have very strange and mixed ideas about love. There are those who mistakenly think it is purely a physical thing. They engage in all sorts of illicit and immoral acts in the name of what they continually tell themselves is love. It becomes immediately clear to anyone who reads the Bible with a mind that wants answers that this is not what the Bible means by love. THE LOVE THAT THE BIBLE SPEAKS OF AS BEING THE GREATEST—IS NEVER SELFISH, IRRESPONSIBLE, NOR IMMORAL.

2. Richard L. Strauss, *Confident Children and How They Grow* (Wheaton, Illinois: Tyndale Publishers, 1975) Adapted.

WITHOUT LOVE ... THE THINGS THAT HAPPEN IN LIFE — WILL BEAT ME.

LOVE HAS GOT TO COME FIRST IN SUCCESSFUL LIVING. WITHOUT LOVE, YOU ARE NOTHING, I AM NOTHING, THE WORLD IS NOTHING. If it were possible to sum up the teachings of Christ in one word, it would be LOVE.

The Apostle Paul begins I Corinthians 13 by stating that without love, "I am nothing." If a person is a nothing, he is a nobody. That is the opposite of being a somebody. A nobody is of no worth to himself or to anyone else. I must admit that without love, I am a nobody. The times when my life rises in value is when I have love. There is not a greater feeling of self-worth than when I am giving and receiving love. LOVE IS ACCELERATING! NOT ONLY DOES IT MAKE ME FEEL THE BEST, BUT IT BRINGS THE BEST OUT IN ME!

Dr. Robert Schuller, in his book "Self-Love" tells this story. "Here is how George Smith tells his story: 'I locked the door to my office. Never had I felt so low as I did when I turned my back on the door of my broken dreams. I walked slowly to the parking lot, got into my car and headed for home. Oh, God, it was all I had left! I stepped into the house. I expected to hear my wife call out, 'Is that you, dear?' I heard nothing. I walked to the kitchen and found a note: 'I've gone shopping. Be home late.' I sank into a chair, a crushed human being.

Suddenly, the door opened. It was my little girl, home from school. She put her lunch box on the table, spotted me and called, 'Daddy! How come you're home so early?' I answered, 'Well, honey, Daddy is changing jobs, but let's not talk about it now, okay?' Then my daughter jumped on my lap, hugged me tight around the neck, pressed her soft and warm face against my face, and gave me the warmest, sweetest kiss, saying, 'Oh, Daddy, I love you so much!' That did it! I really cracked up. My lips quivered. She said, 'What's wrong, Daddy?' I said, 'Nothing, honey, nothing at all. There's absolutely nothing wrong!'

And I really meant it! In that moment, I discovered that I *had* what I really wanted. Suddenly, my whole life unfolded before me: A young fellow who wanted to be a great success in order to be recognized, in order to feel important, in order to be loved, in order to really respect myself! Well . . . I HAD what I wanted. It was here on my lap! I was loved! And in loving and being loved, I found my sense of self-worth, self-respect and self-dignity.[3]"

Let me confess that no one has failed more in love than I have. I never read I Corinthians Chapter 13 without realizing how many times I have fallen short of God's kind of love. THE NAME OF THE CHRISTIAN GAME IS—TO RECEIVE GOD'S CHOICE LOVE GIFT AND BECOME A CHRISTIAN—THEN GROW IN LOVE INTO EVERYTHING THAT NAME MEANS.

Today I again read these words in I Corinthians 14:1, "Let love be your greatest aim." (TLB) My heart responds to that challenge. Yes, Lord, more than the ability to speak, more than having great knowledge, more than making money, more than getting ahead, more than doing things to get people's attention, I want to love Your way!

17

3. Dr. Robert H. Schuller, *Self-Love: The Dynamic Force Of Success*, (New York: Hawthorne Books, 1969) p. 22-23.

WITHOUT LOVE I AM BEATEN

Once again, Bill was in jail. As I visited with him through the iron bars, he said, "I am a loser." As I thought about these defeating words later, I remembered how this man had shut God's love out of his life. From everything I had seen, this repeating law breaker didn't love anyone—least of all himself—and without love, he was a loser; not once, but again and again.

LOVE MINUS LOVE
EQUALS ZERO!

Otis Skilling, in his musical entitled Love, has written these words:
"Love can change the attitude;
Love can change the mind.
Love can make us likeable;
Love can make us kind.
Love can break the barriers;
Love can set us free.
In other words, love can mold
A new life for you and me.[4]"

The sign over the door read "St. John's Christian Book Center." As I walked inside, I had the feeling that this was a good place to be. The store was roomy, and yet it was done in warm light colors. The latest books were displayed in a way that said— "Take me home!"

18

---

4. From the musical, "Love" (Kansas City, Missouri: Lillenas Publishing Company, © 1971). Used by permission.

The lady behind the counter gave the appearance of being in her early fifties. She was fashionably dressed in exquisite taste. That day, I met in person, Dorothy L. Turnbull, an amazing lady!

Here is why I believe Dorothy is an amazing lady. Three years ago, her husband, who owned a lumber brokerage, was attacked in his office by hoods acting like animals. It wasn't enough for them to loot the office and rob the innocent victim, but for no apparent reason, they murdered Mr. Turnbull by stabbing him to death.

It is shattering enough to lose one's mate in death, but to have him unjustly murdered is a nightmare beyond description. With a smile on her face, Dorothy told me how God had used this horrible experience to bring her family so much closer to Him, and to each other.

After months of meditating and trying to pick up the pieces, and put her life back together, God gave her a life-changing idea. A way that she could turn hate into love, tragedy into triumph, tears into joy. In the St. John's area, there was a great need for the witness of a Christian book center. It is an area with the highest crime rate. Dorothy didn't just put in a book store. She has invested assets from her husband's business, and put in a magnificent store. She is God's missionary in an area just a short distance from where her husband was murdered. When I asked her, "Why here?" she said, "It was here where the greatest need was." Here is a lady who is winning with love. You can overcome evil with good. You can turn hate into love. LOVE IS THE GREATEST—GOD'S KIND OF LOVE WILL BRING THE GREATEST OUT OF YOU! SO,

OPEN UP WIDE TO RECEIVE THE LOVE THAT
GOD HAS JUST FOR YOU!

BECAUSE ...
GOD'S KIND OF LOVE
WINS
AGAIN
AND
AGAIN!

CHAPTER 2

Whoever Said
It Was Easy to Love?

Have you ever found yourself engrossed in someone else's conversation, and then felt a little embar-. rassed when you realized that you shouldn't be eavesdropping? Well, I had that experience the other day in a Discount Store. Two men dressed in work clothes were talking like old friends to each other. The larger man, dressed in soiled overalls, said, "That . . . . boss of mine is a stupid fathead! He is constantly yelling at everyone. No matter how hard I work, it is impossible to please him. He is, without a doubt, the most overbearing, crabby person, I have ever known. He's the kind of a person that only a mother could love, and I think that she'd have a pretty hard time of it!"

As C.W. Vendenbergh has said:
"To love the whole world
To me is no chore;
My only real problem's
My neighbor next door."

WHOEVER SAID IT WAS EASY TO LOVE? IS IT EASY TO LOVE . . .

A person who mistreats one of your children?
The big kid next door who gave your kid a black eye?
Your mate when an opinion differs from yours?
When you are exhausted and don't feel well?
When you are doing business for a profit?
When a person takes advantage of you?
When a member of your family has been raped?
When you finally find an empty parking spot, and just as you are about to park, someone beats you to it?
When a person you like a lot says something that hurts you?
When your mate has been unfaithful?

*FACE IT—LOVE IS
THE NAME OF THE CHRISTIAN GAME!*

Admittedly, to practice love all of the time is humanly impossible. As Charlie Brown might say in the cartoon *Peanuts*, "It's hard enough to love when it's easy!" The majority of human beings find it impossible to practice love towards an enemy.

Let's face it—just to practice love towards those we love is hard enough. We simply don't seem to have enough love to go around!

IT IS MAN'S FAILURE TO PRACTICE LOVE THAT RESULTS IN SO MUCH OF OUR WORLD'S HEARTBREAK: WARS
DIVORCES
SEPARATIONS
LONELINESS
EMOTIONAL ILLNESS

Where can we get that vital supply of love that successful living demands? WE MUST GO TO GOD —WHO IS THE SOURCE—"GOD IS LOVE." "For God so loved the world . . . that He gave His only begotten Son . . ." GOD PROVED HIS LOVE FOR US—"by sending Christ to die for us while we were yet sinners." (Romans 5:8, TLB) According to the Bible, and my own experience, when a person receives Jesus Christ as personal Lord and Savior, he receives God's love. Hear what the scripture says in Romans 5:5, "And we feel this warm love everywhere within us, because God has given us His Holy Spirit to fill our hearts with His love." THE MORE WE ARE FILLED WITH GOD'S LOVE—THE MORE WE ARE ABLE TO LOVE OURSELVES AND OTHERS!

In many situations you and I experience, it seems utterly impossible that we can act in love. But the wondrous truth is that with Jesus Christ as Lord, and with His Spirit in control of our lives—the impossible becomes the possible! I like the words of Eugenia Price:

"The giving of God-love is always possible, because, as Jesus said,'With God all things are possible.'We do not admit our own weaknesses when we fail to love,we simply admit our own stubborn refusal to permit God to be Himself in us.[1] "

Can you imagine the pain and grief that would come to a man who was actually married to a harlot? Hosea, the chosen Prophet of God was married to a woman who became a harlot. Sin is unfaithfulness. When one ceases to love God, and turns himself to follow other paths, he is guilty of this tragic sin. Again and again Hosea's wife broke his heart as she went and slept with strange men. Finally, her degradation went so far that she ended up being sold as a slave, to be used as a thing, at the will of men.

What love Hosea possessed in spite of his wife's repeated adultery, lack of response to his love, and desertion. This constant love for his wife was unstoppable. The kind of love that the prophet practiced was so unlike shallow human love and so much like God's deep love. Hosea actually sold everything he had turning it into cash so he could buy his woman back. He took delight in redeeming his beloved, purifying her, and restoring her as the queen in their home and sweetheart in his life! The unconditional love that we see displayed in the life of the prophet, Hosea, is strange indeed to us.

Hosea was an unusual human being, who helps us to catch the picture of what God's unconditional love is like. God loves each of us in a way that we never even dreamed was possible. Nothing about us stops Him from loving us!

LOVE IS THE NAME OF THE CHRISTIAN

1. Eugenia Price, *Make Love Your Aim* (Grand Rapids, Michigan: Zondervan Publishing Co., 1967) p. 155.

GAME. "Dear Friends, let us practice loving each other, for love comes from God. Those who are loving and kind show that they are the children of God, and that they are getting to know Him better. But if a person isn't loving and kind, he shows that he doesn't know God—for God is love." (I John 4:7-8, TLB)

On a recent Sunday afternoon, as I was looking through the Friendship and Communication Cards which our Sunday worshippers fill out, I came across Wanda's hospital visit request.

For many years, Wanda had not had much contact with her father and stepmother, who lived in California. Then, last spring, came the glorious news that her prayers had been answered: Her father had become a new person in Christ Jesus! A couple of months ago, Wanda's father and stepmother moved to Sutherlin. Our church family has been rejoicing with Wanda over this closer family relationship. WHAT A DIFFERENCE THE LOVE OF JESUS MAKES!

The joy of reunion was dampened this week when Wanda's stepmother was admitted to the Good Samaritan Hospital, and then her father also became a patient in the same hospital.

Monday morning, while I was sitting at my desk doing my planning, the telephone rang. It was Wanda. She said, "Pastor, could you possibly go see my stepmother today? She is in a lot of pain, and she has just heard that my father might have a malignant tumor in his throat. Evelyn really needs a spiritual uplift." You can bet on it, when I receive an urgent call, such as this one, I reschedule everything else and go. YOU SEE, LOVING SERVICE ISN'T

ALWAYS CONVENIENT!

I took the elevator to the third floor, walked down the corridor and walked into the room where Evelyn was. This dear lady's pain was so intense that she was sitting up in bed, holding her head in her hands, and gently sobbing. At the moment it seemed to her that the physical pain, compounded with her worry about her husband's condition, was overwhelming. As we talked about Jesus and prayed together, the strength and awareness of Jesus' very presence came into her room.

In glowing terms, Evelyn told me how the night before, being a long way from home and friends, she felt very lonely until God sent a very special person to visit her. She had never met her beautiful Christian visitor before, although they had in common the experience of having been married to the same man. Evelyn could not get over the fact that her husband's ex-wife, of twenty years ago, Wanda's mother, had come to visit her and show her Christian friendship and love.

I cannot imagine that it was easy for Wanda's mother to go and make this visit, but I am sure that she is being rewarded many times for the love she has given. CHRISTIAN LOVE ISN'T ALWAYS AN EASY THING TO GIVE—BUT IT WINS AGAIN AND AGAIN.

THE REAL TEST AS TO THE VALIDITY OF SAYING WE ARE CHRISTIANS IS HOW WE LOVE. "By this all men will know that ye are my disciples, if you have love for one another," said Jesus. (John 13:35, KJV)

LEARNING TO LOVE
IS OUR GREATEST CHALLENGE.

Some people find it difficult to express love to anyone—even those in their families. This may stem from the fact that they were brought up in a home where little or no love was shown. At times, everyone finds it difficult to love. There are people who are hard to love. LET'S FACE IT—NOT EVERYONE IS LOVABLE LIKE YOU AND ME!

I don't imagine that Jesus found it easy to love His enemies. In His earthly manhood, He was tempted in all points as we are. (Hebrews 2:18) He was tempted, no doubt, to withhold His love from those who are cruel, unjust, arrogant, and hateful. Yet, love was so dominant and strong in Jesus that He did not yield to temptation, but plunged ahead courageously to show love in the most impossible of human situations. WHAT A LEADER IN LOVE JESUS IS!

YOU CAN COUNT ON IT—LOVE WINS AGAIN AND AGAIN! But before you can win with love, you must become a follower of Jesus, and allow Him to teach you how to love. How different is God's way for us to live. Did you know that no Christian is ordinary—he is a child of God! Beyond this, as we learn to practice Christ's love in daily living, our living becomes extraordinary.

WHERE JESUS IS
THERE IS LOVE!!

WHO NEEDS TO LEARN HOW TO PRACTICE LOVE? I do, and so do you, for we are all guilty of failing to love. Let's ask the people you live with if you have any need to learn better how to love. Paul said, "My prayer for you is that you will overflow more and more with love for others . . . " (Philippians 1:9) HEAR THIS—HEAR THIS—WHEN IT COMES TO LEARNING HOW TO LOVE—YOU ARE NOT:

    TOO OLD TO LEARN

    TOO BIG A FAILURE TO LEARN

    TOO HELPLESS TO LEARN

    TOO GOOD TO LEARN

    TOO ADVANCED TO LEARN

BEING A DISCIPLE MEANS—BEING A *LEARNER!*

HERE ARE THREE THINGS THAT YOU CAN DO TO HELP YOURSELF BECOME A MORE LOVING INDIVIDUAL:

1. ACCEPT THE FACT THAT YOU ARE A PERSON GOD LOVES! More times than not when we are grumpy, irritable, nagging, and fault-finding, it is a symptom that we are unhappy with ourselves. How miserable that lack of self-appreciation makes us. A lack of self-love makes human beings do the most hateful things to other persons.

In the classic book *The Greatest Thing In The World*, Henry Drummond tells this story:

"Edward Irving went to see a dying boy once, and when he entered the room he just put his hand on the sufferer's head, and said, 'My boy, God loves you,' and went away. The boy started from his bed, and called out to the people in the house, 'God loves me/ God loves me!'[2]"

That one magic word, "love," changed him from a sick boy to a well boy. WHAT TRANSFORMING MIRACLES HAPPEN TO THOSE WHO RECEIVE THE LOVE OF GOD!

28

2. Henry Drummond, *The Greatest Thing In The World* (Carmel, New York: Guideposts Associates, Inc., 1974) p. 19.

Today there are people who, yesterday, berated themselves with self-hatred and bathed in self-pity. The result was that they had trouble loving anyone. But now they have gotten a transfusion of God's love and they are being set free from selfishness to love others. If they would testify this day, they would tell you that their miracle began the moment they accepted themselves as a person whom God loves. It is true—you, too, will be more loving the moment you accept the fact that you are a person whom God loves! SO WISE UP—LOVE WHAT GOD LOVES!

2. MAKE IT A HABIT TO STOP AND THINK FOR ONE MINUTE BEFORE YOU REACT. Ask yourself these all-important questions:

Do I want to be like him, or worse?

Do I want to make this situation worse than it is?

Do I want to act like a Christian or a non-Christian?

Remember, the only person who can make you act in an unloving, unchristian way is YOU! You, more than anyone else, determine the state of your emotions.

TELL YOURSELF THIS TRUTH—THIS EMOTIONAL CRISIS IS MY GREATEST OPPORTUNITY, WITH CHRIST'S HELP, TO SHOW OTHER PEOPLE WHAT REAL, CHRISTIAN LOVE IS LIKE. LET LOVE FLOW!

*LOVE IS SOMETHING YOU DO
REGARDLESS OF HOW YOU FEEL!*

As Professor James said:
"Emotions are not subject to reason
but always subject to action."

3. PRACTICE LOVE WHETHER YOU FEEL LIKE IT OR NOT. People who run their lives by their emotions are like a train trying to be run by the caboose. You sit around waiting until you have good feelings before you act in love toward others. You are going to stop love cold! Christian love is not fondness, it is not how you feel, it is what you do. Yes, love is something you do regardless of how you feel. You do it, not because you feel like it, but because it is the right thing to do. Set your will to love, and your emotions will come along. AS WE PRACTICE LOVE—A MIRACLE HAPPENS—WE BECOME MORE LOVING!

Set your will
Make love your practice and
Your emotion will turn to love!

IT MAY NOT BE EASY TO LOVE
BUT IT SURE HAS MULTIPLE REWARDS!

LOVE IS THE HEALTHIEST, HAPPIEST AND GREATEST WAY TO LIVE! Living and giving love:
Make one a recipient of God's promises.
Bring out the best of us and others.
Make us attractive to others.
LOVE WILL BRING US TOGETHER!
In my book, *Dream A New Dream*, I relate this true, personal experience: "Yesterday evening I

arrived home, went into the bedroom to change my clothes, and happened to glance out the window, and two feet from my window stood a young boy. Fifteen feet behind him stood huge blackberry bushes from which we have enjoyed eating for the last couple of weeks. There, right in the middle of the bushes, on top of our picnic table, were two other kids, uninvited. These invaders had trespassed into our privacy. I knocked on the window, got their attention, opened the window, and yelled to them to please leave, and not to pick the blackberries anymore without our permission. They looked at me as if I were 'Mr. Bad Guy,' said some unrepeatable things, and finally made their way home. A few minutes later, they were back with their mother. The mother wanted to know why I had to be so hostile, and not let her children pick blackberries. After she left, I felt just terrible inside. I did not want to have bad feelings with our new neighbors. All these emotions, the strained relationship with the neighbor, were just eating me up inside.

I decided to do something about it. As Christ's follower, I was to be an example of love in action. I made my way across the field, and knocked on the door. The lady came to the door, and called her children. I took my opportunity to very kindly and very diplomatically explain to the mother, in front of her children, exactly what had happened as I saw it. I then concluded by saying, 'FRIENDSHIP IS MORE IMPORTANT THAN BERRIES.' I didn't really mind the children picking the berries. It was their trespassing on our privacy that I did not like. But I wanted to be their friend, and I wanted them to be my friends, and then I smiled. As it ended up, the children apologized, I apologized, everybody felt good, and everyone was friendly! LOVE WON THE DAY!"[3]

LOVE WINS AGAIN AND AGAIN!

Several years ago, I read *The Seed Must Die*. It is the story of a Korean pastor who went through the atrocities of the Second World War, and was in prison most of his life. He was released from prison, and along with his two sons, established a new ministry in Korea. Soon after the war, the Communists began their uprising, and in those early days, it wasn't military action as much as it was student revolution. In one of the riots his two sons were shot by the Communists. The response from the dear pastor was unbelievable. They caught some of those whom they thought had done the deed, and as it was in the early days of the Communist movement in Korea, they were put on trial to be punished. As the pastor, whose sons were killed, was wrestling with the problem, he wrote to Christian friends in the city where the trial was being held:

"When the people of a country fight against each other who can tell where it will end?", he wrote. "Each side will take revenge on the other, and this could go on until almost all are destroyed. The tide of revenge must be checked. Let someone go at once to Pastor Duk Whan in Soon Chun and tell him, 'Those who killed my sons, if they are found, must not be beaten or put to death. I wish to adopt them as my sons.' "

Only one of the boys was found to be guilty, and it

32

3. Dale E. Galloway, *Dream A New Dream* (Wheaton, Illinois: Tyndale Publishers, 1975) p. 74-75.

is a thrilling story to see the way this one who killed the boys was kept from death by the angry people. He became part of the family of the pastor. The sister of the two martyred brothers became a sister to the man who killed them.

It is a most remarkable story. Beautifully, the writer shows the inner turmoil that goes on in the lives of these Christians. It is almost a year before the boy finally responds and is converted, but in the next to the last paragraph of the book, the son writes to his father from a Bible School:

"Please don't be worried about me. I study the Bible, pray, join in the singing, and do some preaching. Please pray for me. I know I owe everything to you—your prayers and others. As your eldest son, I shall use every means of growing in the spiritual life. And, Father, please forgive me for everything. Because of your love given me by God, I shall try to fulfill your desires for me and shall attempt to follow in the footsteps of St. Paul. I shall do all in my power to follow after the example of my two brothers.[4]"

It is not God's will for us to live negatively, to retreat and to become occupied with our own hurts to the exclusion of all else. Ours is the highest of challenges—to be the salt of the earth, making men thirsty for God's love. Love is your most rosy possibility. As God's own child you have been chosen to live creatively and positively by putting love into action. It is your opportunity to bring Christ's love to bear in some of the most distressing situations that life has to offer. Sound impossible? It is! But with Christ I can do all things. I can act in a loving way when I don't feel loving.

LOVE IS SOMETHING YOU DO—NO MATTER

4. From *The Seed Must Die* by Yong Coon Ahn. © by Inter-Varsity Fellowship, London, and used by permission of Inter-Varsity Press, Downers Grove, IL 60515.

WHAT OTHERS DO. I don't know about you, but my greatest desire is to be known as a man who loves. YOU SEE—THAT'S WHAT BEING A CHRISTIAN MEANS!

CHAPTER 3

Wipe Out Hate With Love!

DO YOU KNOW WHAT THE TWO MOST POWERFUL FORCES ARE IN THE WORLD TODAY? These two opposing forces are in heavy competition at this very moment.

> One brings people together, while the other drives people apart.
> One helps, while the other hurts.
> One is healthy, while the other is unhealthy.
> One is God, while the other is the devil.

THEY ARE: LOVE AND HATE.

One of the things which I have discovered is that

you can usually tell which one, love or hate, is dominating a person's life by the sound of their voice. I remember hearing the story of a man who had a flat tire on a country road while it was raining. He was all dressed up in his best clothes, and late for an appointment. The upset man got his jack out, and crawled underneath the car in the mud and rain. He was jacking up the car when a farmer came by and said, "Do you have a flat tire?" That was a dumb question to ask, and it was obvious to anyone, especially to the stranded man, that he had a flat tire. Why did the farmer ask such a senseless question? He wanted to help the man in his time of need, but first he wanted to hear the sound of the man's voice, to see if the man was so angry that he should stay away, or if the man was approachable and would welcome him as a friend. DO YOU KNOW THE VERY SOUND OF YOUR VOICE TELLS WHETHER YOU HAVE LOVE IN YOUR HEART OR HATE?

WHAT IS THE SOUND OF YOUR VOICE TODAY? LOVE DRAWS PEOPLE—HATE DRIVES THEM AWAY. Do you suppose that the multitudes flocked to Jesus because they heard love in His voice, and because they didn't hear this in the other harsh, legalistic religious leaders? Jesus' voice tones said, "I am approachable. I understand. I care. I love you. I will forgive you." LOVE COMPLETELY DOMINATED THE LIFE OF JESUS HERE ON EARTH! What do the people in your home hear in your voice, LOVE OR HATE?

HATE CAN WIPE YOU OUT,
BUT — LOVE — WIPES HATE OUT.

HATE—THE KILLER EMOTION

HATE LITERALLY KILLS OTHER HUMAN BEINGS. It didn't take long for murder to strike in the human family. The very first book of the Bible, Genesis, tells the story of the very first family, Adam's family. Man's first violent act is recorded in the fourth chapter of Genesis. Cain plotted and slew his brother, Abel, in cold blood, and hid his body in the field. What made him act in such an inhuman way? HATE! How do we explain a Hitler who was responsible for having killed millions of innocent Jews? Hate motivated Hitler. How do we account for the endless mass horror and killings that we call wars, which run like an unbroken thread through the pages of history? Hate causes wars. There is never a killing without hate present.

HATE CAN MAKE YOU COMMIT THE CRIME OF MURDER. You say, "I could never take a person's life." I have often said that I could never understand how any thinking, feeling, human being could willfully take the life of another person. How could we be so cruel? Believe me, we have the capacity to be a murderer. You respond, "How ridiculous! I could not kill anyone!" God says, "Whosoever hates his brother is a murderer; and you know no murderer has eternal life." (I John 3:15) The Bible teaches that when you hate another person you already have murder in your heart. HATE IS A DESIRE TO HURT, OR MAKE ANOTHER PERSON PAY. YOU AND I KNOW ALL TOO WELL THAT THERE IS MORE THAN ONE WAY TO MURDER A PERSON. Murder often expresses itself in endless name-calling, dirty tricks, harsh criticism, snubbing another person, trying to destroy the hated person's reputation. YES, HATE CAN CAUSE YOU TO DO SOME VERY UGLY THINGS.

HATE CAN KILL A PERSON . . . KILL HIM INSIDE, WITHOUT A HAND BEING LAID ON HIM. There is no uglier emotion to struggle through life with than hate. HATE IS:

JEALOUS

RUDE

BAD TEMPERED

VINDICTIVE

DISRUPTIVE

MEAN

AND DESTRUCTIVE.

WITH HATE INSIDE—THE PERSON IS ALWAYS OUT OF BALANCE EMOTIONALLY, AND WHEN OUT OF BALANCE, ANYTHING BUT GOOD CAN HAPPEN.

NOT ONLY DOES HATE DISRUPT THE HATER'S EMOTIONAL BALANCE—BUT IT DESTROYS PHYSICAL HEALTH! You cannot harbor hate and feel good physically. As Proverbs 17:22 (TLB) says, "A cheerful heart does good like medicine, but a broken heart makes one sick." A large percentage of physical illness is a direct result of wrong feelings harbored toward another individual. In a meeting of doctors, convened in the eastern part of the United States, there was a bitter rivalry between two nationally known doctors. Each was a very opinionated person, and outspoken as to his own views as being absolutely right. The doctor, whom we will call Dr. Vinson, had a history of heart problems. His own physician had told him repeatedly not to allow himself to get overheated emotionally or he would kill himself. In failing to heed the advice of his own personal physician, he allowed hatred to swell up within him toward the man he saw as his enemy. In the midst of a bitter debate with him on the floor of the convention, with hate in his voice, he made accusations against the other doctor, and suddenly dropped dead on the spot. BELIEVE IT—HATE CAN CHOKE THE VERY LIFE OUT OF YOU.

I HAVE SEEN HATE DESTROY FAMILIES. I once knew a young man who fell deeply in love with a girl of his dreams, and married her. At first, they seemed to be very much in love, but as days and years passed, they had severe money problems, unpaid doctor bills, overdue mortgage payments, and not enough money to pay for all the things he had charged. He allowed his lack of money to embitter his attitude to the point that he stopped showing love to his wife.

This hate that he had toward the circumstances of his own making caused him to become silent and more and more withdrawn. I watched helplessly as this man allowed the hatred to go deeper and deeper within him. When asked the question, "Do you still love your wife?", he would answer "Yes." But his voice tone told the sad story that he had filled his household with hatred. DON'T YOU DO IT—DON'T ALLOW ANY CIRCUMSTANCE, NO MATTER HOW BAD IT APPEARS, TO FILL YOUR HOUSEHOLD WITH HATRED.

GOD'S ANSWER TO HATE IS TO PUT LOVE IN ITS PLACE. That is why Jesus died on a cross—to rid you of hate and to give you love. It is not surprising to find a noted leader in the field of psychiatry like Karl Menninger saying,"Love is the basic need of human nature, for without it, life is disrupted emotionally, mentally, spiritually, and physically." WE HAVE GOT TO HAVE LOVE TO COMBAT HATE. WITHOUT LOVE—GOD'S LOVE—ALL WE HAVE IS HATE—AND THAT IS HELL ON EARTH.

THERE IS NO WAY
YOU CAN AFFORD
TO GIVE HATE A PLACE
WITHIN YOUR HEART!

It was shocking news to hear that our Oregon State Police Chief, Hollie Holcomb, had been murdered on the steps of our capital building in Salem. My first thought was that it was some wild, irrational revolutionary who had assassinated our State Head of Law Enforcement. However, then came the further news that a former Oregon State Policeman, Robert Wampler, had been taken into custody, and charged with the murder.

The media sketched the life of the sixty-two-year-old accused as being a man respected and liked by friends, employees, and neighbors. I looked at the picture of his home, surrounded by towering fir trees, set in the midst of Oregon's finest scenery, and I thought, "What a tranquil looking place to live." I read about the successful cleaners that this man owned and operated, just a few miles from

40

where my wife and I live. Employees and neighbors in disbelief of what happened, told of their own shock that this man, whom they thought a good and generous person, could commit the crime that so many witnesses say they saw him do.

What had happened? What could cause a man who was respected and had all the earthly things it would appear a man wanted, to suddenly erupt in such violence and take the life of another man in cold blood? The story is that seventeen years earlier, Wampler stood for a principle that he thought was right and as a result was discharged from the Oregon State Police. For seventeen years, he continued to tell anyone who would listen to him that he had gotten a raw deal. Richard E. Groener of Milwaukee, former Oregon legislator, who has known Wampler for all these years, said, "The last time I saw him, about a year ago, he was still very, very bitter about his discharge from the Oregon State Police." He said, "I told Bob to forget about being fired, and I tried to convince him to let it go, but he kept saying that he had to exonerate himself of these things. He even asked me to go see the governor to try to get Holcomb fired. He was obsessed with this thing, even after all these years passed."

How tragic that a good man should allow bitterness, over one incident seventeen years ago, to dwell within him until hate exploded and hurt so many people. Hate is always destructive. No matter what someone has done or not done to you, you cannot afford to harbor any bitterness. Bitterness always turns to hate, and hate sooner or later, wipes out everything good.

WHEN YOU HATE SOMEONE, YOU BECOME LIKE HIM OR WORSE. A bitter young father recalled his unhappy childhood days, and affirmed again and again, "One thing for sure, I don't ever want to be like my old man." His dad drank, was unfaithful to his wife, paid no attention to a son who needed a father. Now the son was married and had his own family. He never drank, was faithful to his wife, and spent long hours with his children. Yet, one day his wife blurted out, "You're just like your old man!"

How could this be? When the son kept repeating the statement, "I never want to be like my old man," he established a standard of comparison. The "emotional focus" was on the wrong actions of his old man, and it made it impossible to stop thinking about the man he hated. The more he thought about the misdeeds of his father, the more bitter and hateful he became, until one day his wife looked into his eyes which were filled with hate, and declared, "You're just like your old man." Hate someone, and you will become like them, or worse. FOR WHATEVER GETS YOUR EMOTIONAL ATTENTION, GETS YOU.

WHEN YOU HATE SOMEONE, YOU BECOME THAT PERSON'S SLAVE. The person that you hate can be a thousand miles away, and yet you have to keep thinking about the person you hate. Your negative emotion binds you as a slave. Wherever you go, the thought of hate makes you think about the person. YES, HATING ANOTHER PERSON WILL BIND YOU UP AND MAKE YOU

THAT PERSON'S SLAVE.

GOD WANTS YOU TO BE FREE! The Old Testament tells a very descriptive story about some brothers who were filled with hate. So envious and hateful were Joseph's brothers of his favor with their father, that they sold him into slavery. What cruel mistreatment to receive from the hands of your own brothers. It would have been so easy for Joseph to allow bitterness to take over and fill his personality with hatred. But, although sold into slavery, he refused to be bound by hate. It is absolutely astounding what good God can bring to those who refuse to give hatred a place in their hearts. After many years Joseph was used by God to give food and shelter and life itself, to these same brothers, and to say in love, "You meant it for evil, but God meant it for good." (Genesis 50:20)

OTHERS MAY MISTREAT YOU—BUT REMEMBER, GOD POURS OUT MANY BLESSINGS UPON THOSE WHO CHOOSE LOVE OVER HATE.

GOD BLESSES THOSE WHO REFUSE
TO HAVE ANYTHING TO DO WITH
BITTERNESS—RESENTMENT—OR HATE.

At a gathering of Christians from different denominations I met a beautiful Spanish-American named Samuel. At this small group experience, Samuel related how twelve years ago he and his brother were cast out of their church because they had been filled with the Holy Spirit. It seems that the two brothers both had been wronged and mistreated by their own church family.

43

Now, twelve years later, the one brother who allowed bitterness to take him over is outside of the church and away from God, while Samuel, who refused to allow bitterness to poison his spirit, is being used and blessed of God, as never before, to minister among three hundred Spanish-American families. It is a spiritual principle that those who refuse to become bitter or to hate, no matter how deeply they have been injured by unjust treatment, God blesses them and gives them back so much more than they have lost. To God be the glory for the great things He does for those who allow His love to wipe out all hate.

HATE IS LIKE A FISH HOOK
ONCE IT GETS HOLD OF YOU
IT KEEPS HURTING UNTIL
YOU GET UNHOOKED.

AS GOD'S CHILDREN OF LOVE, GIVE HATE NO PLACE IN YOUR LIFE. "If anyone says, I love God, but keeps on hating his brother, he is a liar; for if he doesn't love his brother, who is right there in front of him, how can he love God who he has never seen?" (I John 4:20, TLB) CHRISTIAN LOVE IS DIFFERENT FROM ANYTHING THIS WORLD HAS EVER KNOWN. Jesus clearly taught us, by example, that as His followers we are to never attempt any kind of personal revenge. Jesus gave us our example when He was mistreated: "He did not threaten to get even; He left His case in the hands of God, who always judges fairly." (I Peter 2:23, TLB) As a Christian remember what someone once said, "Those who hate you don't win until you hate them back, and that will destroy you."

Jesus gave us very careful instructions on how, as His children, we are to win the victory over hate. Contrary to what some may think, a Christian is not one who lays down while everyone walks on top of him. He is a courageous person who stands up, goes on the offensive, and takes the most positive and forceful action in the world. This is what Jesus said you are to do:

BLESS THEM THAT CURSE YOU,
DO GOOD TO THEM THAT HATE YOU,
PRAY FOR THEM THAT DESPITEFULLY
USE YOU AND PERSECUTE YOU.
THE WAY TO BEAT AN ENEMY
IS TO MAKE HIM A FRIEND:
LOVE WINS A FRIEND
WHEN EVERYTHING ELSE FAILS.

AS GOD'S CHILDREN OF LOVE IT IS UP TO US TO EMPTY OUT ALL HATRED. What do I do when I realize that I have wrong feelings toward another person, when these feelings are bringing out the worst of me? Being a true Christian is being honest. ADMIT IT. ACCEPT THIS TRUTH, THAT NO MATTER WHAT SOMEONE ELSE HAS DONE OR NOT DONE TO YOU, IT IS WRONG FOR YOU TO HAVE HATE TOWARD ANOTHER LIVING PERSON. This is not God's way for you to live. For His children, God has a greater way of love. You have to get the poison of hate out of your system before it does any more damage in your relationships with others and with your God.

OPEN UP TO GOD AND SPILL THE BEANS. Tell Him just how you have been feeling; don't hide anything. God already knows what is inside of you—open up and spill out your hatred. POUR IT OUT—YELL IT OUT—WHISPER IT OUT—DO WHATEVER IT TAKES, BUT—GET IT OUT! YOU'LL NEVER FEEL CLEAN AND FREE UNTIL YOU COME CLEAN WITH YOUR HEAVENLY FATHER. "Create in me a new, clean heart, O God, filled with clean thoughts, and right desires." (Psalm 51:10, TLB)

HAVING CONFESSED IT—NOW ASK GOD TO FORGIVE YOU FOR YOUR SIN. "But if we confess our sins to Him, He can be depended on to forgive us our sins and cleanse us from every wrong." (I John 1:9, TLB) Keeping cleaned up is important to good physical, emotional, and spiritual health. Just as we wash our hands several times a day to keep the germs out of our physical body, we need to let God in His Holy Spirit cleanse us and make us clean on the inside. For good emotional and spiritual health let your heavenly Father cleanse you on the inside again and again. If you have some feelings you haven't been able to rid yourself of, God, your Father, wants to do for you what you cannot do for yourself. OPEN UP AND LET GOD, IN HIS LOVE, CLEAN HATE OUT OF YOUR LIFE. GOD'S LOVE IS THE ONLY THING IN THIS WORLD THAT IS MORE FORCEFUL AND POWERFUL THAN HATE.

WIPE OUT HATE WITH LOVE!

The high point of our Sunday evening, life-centered service, comes when the lights are turned down low and the candles at the front of our sanctuary are lit. At that Holy moment, persons are invited to come to the front and kneel at our Garden of Prayer. What a faith-building experience this is as worshippers draw closer to God and one another. Each Sunday, we open our ten o'clock service with the song, "There's A Sweet, Sweet Spirit in This Place" and each Sunday we end our evening service by experiencing the sweet movement of God's Spirit during our Garden of Prayer. One Sunday night, during the afterglow of this enriching fellowship of God, different ones spontaneously stood to their feet, and in overflowing words of praise, shared the good things Jesus was doing in their lives. VICTORY IN JESUS IS NOT JUST A SONG. IT IS A WAY OF LIFE FOR THOSE WHO ATTEND NEW HOPE!

I was quite surprised when a tall, rather slender lady, in her late twenties, stood to her feet because she had only been attending our services for a few weeks. What a pleasant surprise it was to be in attendance, and hear how God had wiped out hate with love in her life. Listen to the young lady's testimony, as she gave it in her own words:

"Before I started attending New Hope Community Church about a month ago, I hadn't gone to church in more than ten years because I was so full of bitterness that I didn't want anything to do with God. For ten years I have hated the man who murdered my mother. This hatred ruined my first marriage, and would have wiped out my second marriage if I had not been married to such a good man." Here she paused and added meaning to her words by tenderly laying her hand upon the shoulder of her husband as he was seated beside where she was standing. The new convert further described how this ugly hatred she had in her heart against this one man had embittered her and had caused everything in her life to be negative and miserable. WHAT A DEVASTATING TOLL HATRED TAKES ON THOSE WHO HATE.

The happy witness continued: "My sister-in-law started telling me about New Hope and sharing with me what a difference the love of Jesus was making in her own life and marriage. I knew I needed help from somewhere. I sure wasn't enjoying the results of all my hatred, so I decided to attend New Hope's Drive-In Service. There I saw the love that I desperately needed in action.

"After attending for a couple of Sundays, I asked the pastor to come to my home and tell me how I could become a Christian. That night I knelt in my own front room and asked Jesus Christ to come into my life. But you know, the strangest thing has happened to me: I don't hate that man anymore." As she said that, a big smile broke across her face. Then she said, "Look at me. I'm even smiling! That's one thing I haven't done in years!" Those present witnessed that even her face glowed with the love of Jesus. HIS LOVE WILL MAKE YOU GLOW!

GOD'S LOVE CAN WIPE THE HATE OUT OF YOUR LIFE. GOD IS OFFERING YOU HIS TRANSFORMING LOVE RIGHT NOW. GOD'S LOVE TURNS HATE INTO LOVE:
> DIRTY MOUTHS INTO CLEAN ONES,
> ACTING LIKE AN ANIMAL INTO ACTING
>   LIKE A HUMAN BEING,
> ENEMIES INTO FRIENDS,
> A HELL'S ANGEL INTO A CHILD OF GOD.

PRAY THIS PRAYER:

JESUS, I HAVE SINNED. I AM A SINNER.
I ASK YOU TO FORGIVE ME.
THANK YOU FOR DYING FOR ALL MY
SINS AND MY HATE.
I ACCEPT YOU AS LORD AND SAVIOR.
SEND YOUR HOLY SPIRIT OF LOVE INTO
MY HEART
AND MY LIFE, AND FILL ME WITH YOUR
LOVE—
THANK YOU, JESUS!

CHAPTER 4

Worth Loving? That's You!

Right now I want to ask you a very personal question. But first, let me tell you that daily life is set, not by the stars, not by external influence, but by your answer to this all important question. Are you ready? Here it is: What kind of feeling do you have about yourself? WHAT DO YOU THINK OF YOURSELF? DO YOU:

LIKE OR DISLIKE YOURSELF,
RESPECT OR DISRESPECT YOURSELF,
FORGIVE OR NOT FORGIVE YOURSELF,
VALUE OR NOT VALUE YOURSELF,
LOVE OR HATE YOURSELF?

THE MODERN TRAGEDY IS THAT SO MANY PEOPLE DO NOT ENJOY GOOD FEELINGS

ABOUT THEMSELVES. In my pastoral experience, I find that nine out of ten people suffer to a varying degree, from low self-esteem. If you don't love yourself, how can you love anyone else? The answer is: It's pretty difficult—if not impossible! You see, the attitude we have about ourselves colors all our relationships with others. We all know from experience that when we are unhappy with ourselves we are unhappy with everyone else.

One woman confessed, "My family loves me because they are supposed to, but surely no one else could love me." A young person said, "They love me because I do what they want me to, but if I really stood up to the crowd they wouldn't accept me." DO YOU EVER FEEL LIKE YOU ARE AN UNLOVABLE PERSON? I guess a true confession is that at some time all of us have feelings that we are not worth much. These kinds of unworthy feelings are self-defeating. The truth is that when you feel unworthy of love it is not only impossible to give love to others, but it is most difficult to accept love from other people. You always have to read something into their motives. For example, when someone gives you a compliment do you accept it, or do you just pass it off as just idle words?

Someone has penned these words:

"I gave a little tea party this afternoon at three;
'Twas very small, three guests in all—
I, myself, and me.
Myself ate up the sandwiches,
While I drank up the tea.
It was also I that ate the pie,
And passed the cake to me."

51

WHEREVER YOU GO, WITH OTHERS OR ALONE, AS LONG AS YOU ARE ALIVE—YOU HAVE YOURSELF TO LIVE WITH. So wouldn't you agree with me that it is of the utmost significance how you think about yourself? THIS CHAPTER IS TO HELP YOU IMPROVE THE PICTURE THAT YOU HAVE OF YOUR OWN SELF.

GOD THINKS YOU ARE WORTH LOVING
AND HE CAN'T BE WRONG.

Have you ever had the experience of crawling out of bed in the morning, staggering to the bathroom, looking in the mirror, and saying to yourself, "Why didn't God make me good-looking?" Just because you are not the one girl in a million who can win the beauty contest or the big, husky, athletic hero doesn't mean that you are not a beautiful person. BELIEVE ME, THERE IS NO ONE READING THIS IN WHOM GOD HAS NOT PUT BEAUTY WITHIN WHICH HAS YET TO BE DISCOVERED!

GOD, HIMSELF, TAKES DELIGHT IN YOU! Listen to what King David said that God feels for you, His masterwork of all creations:

"You made all the delicate, inner parts of my body, and knit them together in my mother's womb. Thank you for making me so wonderfully complex! It is amazing to think about. Your workmanship is marvelous—and how well I know it. You were there while I was being formed in utter seclusion! You saw me before I was born, and scheduled every day of my life before I began to breathe. Every day was recorded in your book! How precious it is, Lord, to realize that you are thinking about me constantly! I can't even count how many times a day your thoughts turn towards me. And when I waken in the morning, you are still thinking about me!" (Psalm 139:13-18, TLB)

AFTER ALL, IT'S WHAT GOD THINKS
THAT REALLY
COUNTS!

NO MATTER WHAT YOU THINK IS WRONG WITH YOURSELF—GOD BELIEVES YOU ARE WORTH SAVING. "But God showed His great love for us by sending Christ to die for us while we were still sinners." (Romans 5:8, TLB) It would seem that none of us is worthy of such costly love in our behalf. Yet, God gave all His love—for us! Why did He send His son, Jesus, to die on the cross? To save us from our sins! But that isn't all; there is more. Jesus died because God believed that man was worth saving. God saw something there that was wonderful. God wants to eliminate the negative from your life and to bring out the positive. His forgiving and healing touch can cure all your unworthiness. The only shame is in not accepting God's forgiveness and healing. Let Him restore within you, dignity, manhood, and womanhood.

IF YOU WERE THE ONLY
SINNER IN THE WORLD
GOD LOVES YOU SO MUCH,
JESUS WOULD HAVE DIED
TO RESTORE YOUR LOST DIGNITY!

*SIX GOOD REASONS WHY YOU
SHOULD LOVE YOURSELF*

1. THE NUMBER ONE REASON WHY YOU SHOULD LOVE YOURSELF IS—GOD LOVES YOU—AND WHO ARE YOU NOT TO LOVE WHAT GOD LOVES?

2. GOD COMMANDS YOU TO LOVE YOURSELF. Jesus taught that all the rules for the road for a successful journey in life could be summed up in two simple commandments. The first is to love God with all your heart, soul, strength, and mind; and the second is THAT YOU LOVE YOUR NEIGHBOR AS YOURSELF. By these very words Jesus makes it crystal clear that loving ourselves as God's choice creation is crucial to loving others— even the heavenly Father. In the Epistle written to the church at Ephesis, Paul further magnifies our need for self-love, describing God's pattern for the marriage relationship. He says, "So husbands ought also to love their wives as their own bodies." (Ephesians 5:28) The very foundation of a successful marriage is built on the principle of a person accepting his own God-given worth and value and then with clear eyes seeing tremendous worth in his beloved.

3. LOVE YOURSELF OR BE PLAGUED BY JEALOUSY. Jealousy is born out of hatred, not love; first of all, out of self-hatred. All the possessive, jealous people I have known have been convinced that they were not worth loving. It is when we feel worthless that we become jealous, even of loved ones. We have to try to possess them completely in order to tell ourselves that they really care for us. Any interest shown in anyone else; the

slightest friendship displayed toward others is an unbearable threat, confirming the deep suspicions that the other person is really more lovable than we are.

> DON'T COMPARE YOURSELF WITH
> OTHERS.
> GOD DIDN'T MAKE YOU LIKE ANYONE
> ELSE.
> HE MADE YOU UNIQUE,
> SO, STOP TRYING TO BE LIKE ANYONE
> ELSE,
> AND BE YOURSELF!

4. WHEN SELF-LOVE IS LACKING IT BECOMES QUITE EASY TO BECOME CRITICAL AND JUDGMENTAL OF OTHERS. We judge them harshly out of our own inferior concept of ourselves. The more people feel beaten down the more they try to beat others down to their own level. The only problem is it doesn't help. It just makes things worse! The more you run someone down the crummier you are going to feel about yourself.

5. YOU SHOULD LOVE YOURSELF TO BE FREE FROM SELFISHNESS. When self-love is lacking, you will find yourself slipping back into being selfish—no matter how hard you try not to be. You see, when one is dissatisfied with himself he has to keep thinking of himself all of the time. Thinking of yourself as a miserable person locks you into a negative focus. The way to get loose from self-centeredness—the way to be free—is simple. Accept God's love, love yourself, then love others!

SELFISHNESS AND SELF-LOVE,
FAR FROM BEING IDENTICAL,
ARE ACTUALLY OPPOSITES.[1]

6. SELF-LOVE WILL HELP YOU TO BE
SECURE ENOUGH THAT SOMEONE'S NEGA-
TIVE REMARK ABOUT YOU WILL NOT WIPE
YOU OUT. Sometimes a single negative or deflating
remark can do enormous damage to a person's belief
in himself. A story that I read somewhere years ago
that was shared by the famous novelist, A.J. Cronin
out of his own experience illustrates this. He said
that as a young medical student (he was a doctor
before he was a writer) he had a professor of
surgery who was harsh and outspoken and critical.
One day, this man stopped Cronin in the hall and
told him that his performance was hopeless, that he
might be an adequate general practitioner, but that
he would never be a surgeon. And Cronin believed
him.

But then, the young doctor went to a remote
village in the Scottish highlands to practice. He was
the only physician for miles around. One winter's
day, with roads blocked by snow and ice, a tree fell
on the son of the local pastor crushing his spine and
paralyzing him. Cronin knew that an operation was
imperative; without it, the paralysis would be
permanent. But he remembered what the professor
had said and he was afraid to take the risk because
the slightest mistake could mean death for the boy.

The pastor himself urged Cronin to operate. He
would pray for him, he said. God would help him.
Cronin kept refusing. He said, "All I could think of,
was the face of that man telling me that I could
never be a surgeon."

56

1. Robert Schuller, *Self Love: The Dynamic Force of Success*, (New York:
Hawthorne Books, Inc., 1969) p. 42.

But then something happened. Cronin described it as a sudden surge of anger. "For the first time," he said, "I questioned the validity of that man's verdict. Who was he to tell me what I could or couldn't do? A kind of fury came over me and swept away the doubts and fears. I knew I could operate successfully. And with God's help, I did!" THERE ARE MANY THINGS YOU MAY THINK YOU CANNOT DO—BUT WITH GOD'S HELP—YOU CAN DO!

TREAT YOURSELF LIKE SOMEONE WORTH LOVING!

Under God's direction Moses told the Jewish father to tell his little son at the tent door every evening that he was a child of God. DO YOURSELF A TREMENDOUS FAVOR—CLAIM YOUR SON-SHIP! "As many as received Him, to them gave He power to become the sons of God, even to them that believe on His name." (John 1:12)

SEE HOW VERY MUCH
OUR HEAVENLY FATHER
LOVES US
FOR HE ALLOWS US TO BE CALLED
HIS CHILDREN
THINK OF IT—AND WE REALLY ARE!
WHAT COULD BE GREATER THAN
TO BECOME A CHILD OF GOD!

TREAT YOURSELF RIGHT BY LIVING RIGHT. After years of working with scores of people I can tell you first hand that there is nothing that destroys self-respect like sin. You have to live with yourself and when you have done what you know is wrong, that can be tough! Sin may be fun for a fleeting moment but it will do anything but build your self-esteem. As Janis Joplin has appropriately said:

"YOU BETTER NOT COMPROMISE YOURSELF IT'S ALL YOU HAVE."

Would you like to know a little secret about this pastor? Well, the inside dope is that on Mondays, following my big day on Sunday, I am out of gas emotionally. I feel emotionally like I used to feel physically in my high school days after playing a big football game . . . zapped! Contrary to a majority of ministers I like to take Saturdays off, to be with my family, but make it a habit to work on Mondays. I use Monday to do administrative work and planning but try to keep it as one of the lighter work days in my week.

On a Monday several months ago, I was hit with unbelievably heavy emotional demands on my already depleted energies. In the course of the day I took care of some heavy administrative responsibilities at the office; comforted a frightened member facing surgery in the hospital; spent several hours at the court house with one of my families who were involved in an emotionally taxing and tearing custody suit; counseled with a man on the brink of utter despair and hopelessness; went through battle with a couple who were teetering between reconciliation and splitting the sheets.

By four o'clock in the afternoon I was so emotionally drained that I could hardly hold my head up, but was taking strength from the thought that I would soon be away from all the grief and pain that people bear and inflict to spend a relaxing evening in the happy solitude of our home.

Just then, the phone rang and the lady at the other end, in an anxious voice, said, "Pastor, could you possibly see my husband?" I picked up my appointment book and looked at it and suggested to her that I make an appointment to see her husband in my office Wednesday afternoon. I asked her if that would be satisfactory. In a voice of urgency this woman, whom I judged to be a very calm person, pleaded with me that I might see her husband yet today. In tears she told me that he had been contemplating suicide and he'd come to the end of himself where he realized that his only hope was in God. I told the dear lady that I would gladly see her husband as soon as she could drive him to my office. As I hung up the phone God's Spirit gave me a new surge of emotional energy. Someone must have been praying for their pastor!

Soon Charles and his wife were seated in my office. I noticed right away that Charles did not like himself, nor did he think that anyone else liked him. So low was his opinion of himself that he found it impossible to sit and look at me directly. Because of a handicap he hated his own physical appearance. Each day as he watched his wife go to work and earn the living, while he stayed at home, he had hated himself more and more, until, in his own eyes, he had become a contemptible person. He sought relief in alcohol but it only added to his own mental torment.

Charles told me that he wanted to be a Christian. I took the Bible and went through the steps to

59

becoming a Christian with my new friend. I asked him if, more than anything else, he wanted to become a child of God. He said that he did and together we went into the sanctuary to kneel and pray. I helped him pray a simple prayer of commitment, but to his tormented self, there came no relief or peace. The Spirit prompted me and I asked him directly when he was going to stop feeling sorry for himself and told him that self-pity was one luxury he could not afford. It almost sounds cruel, now, but I told him to stop hating himself. In bitter words the self-hatred and contempt that he felt poured out like a dam that had broken. Then I said to my friend, "Right now give yourself, as unacceptable as you feel that you are, to God. He wants you just as you are." And in a simple prayer he gave his unacceptable self to God. It was then that Charles made the wonderful discovery that God loved Charles and accepted him as His own son!

Now having accepted Jesus Christ into his life and claiming his sonship as a child of God, Charles is learning to appropriate God's love, forgiveness, peace, and acceptance. And with this love, that is God's, he is beginning to see himself as a person worth loving!

WHAT A NEW PERSPECTIVE COMES WHEN WE BECOME A CHILD OF GOD! The self-contempt is gone from his eyes and now he is beginning to see himself as God sees him. The deeper view, not the surface one, as a person of value and great worth in God's sight. NO MATTER WHAT PHYSICAL MARKS, SCARS, OR HANDICAPS YOU MIGHT HAVE, YOU TOO, ARE A PERSON WORTH LOVING!

In Dr. Robert Schuller's classic book on Self-Love, he illustrates self-love, as being true to your highest ideals, with this impact story:

"A young man shared this with me. I was bored one night and went to a neighborhood bar. I met this chick and we started drinking. She was lonely. I was unmarried. She was divorced. 'Let's go to Las Vegas,' she suggested. I looked at the hungry invitation in her sultry eyes and immediately put my glass down, paid the bartender, took her arm and headed for her car. She snuggled warmly and hungrily close to me. We roared through the night with visions of a hot bed in a Vegas motel. For some strange reason which I cannot explain, I was suddenly gripped by the thought that this was a pretty cheap thing for me to do. I found myself mentally torn at the sexual compulsion to 'shack up' with this barfly for whom I had no respect whatsoever. At the same time, glancing in the rear-view mirror, I saw my own eyes. They were the eyes of a potentially wonderful person. I was beginning to feel the disgust and self-loathing that I had known on more than one occasion after indulging in a depersonalizing sexual escapade. I pulled over to the shoulder of the road and stopped the car. 'What are you doing?' she asked.

" 'I'm getting out, ' I answered abruptly. 'It's your car. Go on to Vegas if you want to. I don't care what you do. I'll thumb a ride back.' I slammed the door shut and watched as she angrily spun the wheels in the gravel and roared furiously away. I stood there alone in the night on a lonely stretch of desert road. Suddenly I felt ten feet tall! I never felt so good in my life! I felt like a triumphant general returning victoriously from a proud battle. That was my moment of self-love.[2] "

You can't live like a pig and feel much self-worth. Our biggest problem is that we have to live with ourselves. Aren't you glad that Christ has a way of helping us to live so we can be true to our highest ideals and feel like we are really worth something.

TREAT YOURSELF WITH CHRISTIAN LOVE BY SEEING THAT YOU ARE NOT PERFECT, BUT IN THE PROCESS OF BECOMING. A Christian, yes, but also growing into that name! A breath of fresh air came into the young lady's life when she realized that she did not have to be perfect in performance to be a good Christian. Jesus Christ accepts us where we are and says—let's go from here to become the person of beauty I have created you to be. LET JESUS' LIFE AND SPIRIT BREATHE AND BLOOM WITHIN YOU. WITH THIS IN MIND DO THESE THREE THINGS:

1. LIVE IN THE PRESENT—NOT IN THE PAST.
2. FORGIVE YOURSELF—IT'S THE ONLY DECENT THING TO DO.
3. SEE YOURSELF IN THE BEST POSSIBLE LIGHT—THINK OF YOUR GOOD POINTS WHILE, WITH CHRIST'S HELP, WORKING TO IMPROVE YOUR BAD POINTS.

In a recent fellowship of Christians a young mother shared how, after not sleeping well one night, she woke up somewhat grumpy in the morning. Right off the bat one of her children spilled her milk. Then another one spilled her milk. Before

62

2. Robert Schuller, *Self-Love: The Dynamic Force of Success*, (New York: Hawthorne Books, Inc., 1969) p. 34-35.

the mother knew it she was back into an old habit pattern of yelling.

Having overheard the ruckus, her husband came into the kitchen and quietly said, "It sounds like we are back in the old house." She wisely got the point and apologized for her relapse.

Later, this Christian lady reflected on what had occurred. There came the sweet realization to her that her husband, whom she hopes will someday attend church with her, sees the difference that Christ is making in her and he likes it.

THIS IS YOUR PROMISE, "AND I AM SURE THAT GOD, WHO BEGAN THE GOOD WORK WITHIN YOU, WILL KEEP RIGHT ON HELPING YOU GROW IN HIS GRACE UNTIL HIS TASK WITHIN YOU IS FINALLY FINISHED ON THAT DAY WHEN JESUS CHRIST RETURNS." (Philippians 1:6, TLB)

TREAT YOURSELF TO SUCCESS BY DISCOVERING THE GREATNESS THAT IS ALREADY PLANTED WITHIN YOU . . . One might hold a seed in his hand and make the comment, "It isn't much." But no statement could be further from the truth. For what mighty potential for a bountiful harvest is already present within this tiny seed. What seeds of tremendous possibilities God has already planted within you!

JESUS PUT HIS FINGER ON YOUR UNDISCOVERED POSSIBILITIES FOR SERVICE TO HIS KINGDOM WHEN HE SAID: "You are the salt of the earth . . . You are the light of the world."

TO JESUS YOU ARE A SOMEBODY . . . WHO HAS A LOT TO GIVE TO OTHERS!

Cavett Robert, in his Personal Development Course, tells this story:

A father, after observing his five-year-old daughter put her seventh teaspoonful of sugar in her weak tea, could restrain himself no longer. "Darling," he said as he grabbed her hand, "Don't you think that will make your tea too sweet?"

"No, Daddy," she responded sweetly with her impish smile, "Not if you don't stir it.[3]"

How many of us already have within ourselves those qualities that give happiness and success in life which only need stirring? I'm sure that you will agree that it is most regrettable and even tragic to let talent go undeveloped . . . to live with unfulfilled ambitions, unrealized dreams and doors of opportunity that remain unopened so long that the hinges are actually rusty.

3. Cavett Robert, The Cavett Robert Personal Development Course (West Nyack, New York: Parker Publishing Co., 1966).

CHAPTER 5

Love Gifts From Our Father

While having lunch with a friend, he asked me if I had seen the television special the night before about the man who started the American give-away program called Welfare. As the program pointed out no other President of the United States of America has even come close to creating the welfare programs which Franklin D. Roosevelt master-minded.

I guess what one happens to think about Welfare has a great deal to do with whether you are one who receives it or one who pays for it. Although the abuses of Welfare tend to anger every person who works for a living, it does express the tender human emotion of compassion. The Bible tells us clearly that we are to feed the poor, clothe the naked, and give to those who are less fortunate. (See Matthew 25:37-45)

Jesus said, "Inasmuch as ye have done it unto one of the least of these my brethren, ye have done it unto me." (Matthew 25:40)

Better than all man-made welfare programs, God's welfare program:

IS FAIR FOR EVERYONE

BRINGS THE BEST OUT OF ITS
PARTICIPANTS

NEVER DESTROYS HUMAN INITIATIVE
AND DIGNITY, BUT ENCOURAGES IT

MAKES PEOPLE FEEL LOVED AND
SECURE

MEETS THE PROBLEMS OF RISING
INFLATION

IS WITHOUT FAILURES

JUST KEEPS GETTING BETTER AND
BETTER

WHAT AN UNBEATABLE WELFARE
PROGRAM GOD HAS FOR EVERYONE!!

This superior welfare program originated out of God's very nature. What is God like? The Bible says, "GOD IS LOVE" (I John 4:16) Out of His bountiful love, God lavishes good gifts upon all of His children. Jesus said, "If ye being evil know how to give gifts to your children, how much more shall your Father in Heaven give good things to them that ask Him." (Matthew 7:11)

WHAT YOU ARE IS
GOD'S GIFT TO YOU.
WHAT YOU MAKE OF YOURSELF
IS YOUR GIFT TO GOD!

WHAT A NEAT EXPERIENCE IT IS TO SEE A FATHER AND SON WHO HAVE A GOOD RELATIONSHIP WITH EACH OTHER. My wife's cousin, Jerry Watson, has been away from home in the Air Force for the past eleven years. His parents, my wife's Uncle Clayton and Aunt Hazel, have taken us into their immediate family circle and to our delight we get to attend all the family gatherings. Every holiday when the family gathered, feasting and celebrating, the joy would be marred by the same sad note. Uncle Clayton, the head of the Watson clan, would bemoan the fact that his son, Jerry, and his family could not be present.

If there ever was an outdoorsman, who lived to hunt and fish, it is Clayton Watson. Repeatedly during the past eleven years, this father longed for the companionship of his son so that they might enjoy hunting and fishing together. Well, the other day Jerry got out of the service and he brought his wife and two children back home to live. What a time of joyful reunion the family has been celebrating and guess what? Uncle Clayton, the father, and son Jerry are like two little boys anticipating the opening of a candy store. You see, hunting season opens here in Oregon in a few days and they are all revved up, father and son, to go hunting together. It is heartwarming for me to see a father and son who really enjoy each other's company.

Unfortunately, a large number of people for one reason or another do not know what it is to have a good relationship with their own earthly father. But, regardless of whether your relationship with your own father has been fulfilling or disappointing I want you to imagine in your mind right now the most perfect model relationship a son or daughter could possibly have with their earthly father. Having done this, now refine your image to the finest degree of perfection and you begin to catch a glimpse of the perfect flawless relationship Jesus enjoyed throughout His earthly journey with His Heavenly Father. The thing that thrills me is that Jesus taught us that we, too, could actually know God as "Our Father." (Matthew 6:9-13, TLB) Not only does Jesus say that God wants to be our Father, but He urges us not to delay one moment in entering into a rightful son-Heavenly Father relationship, "And so, we should not be like cringing, fearful slaves, but we should behave like God's very own children, adopted into the bosom of His family, and calling to Him, 'Father, Father.' " (Romans 8:15, TLB)

WHAT COULD BE GREATER THAN TO HAVE GOD AS YOUR HEAVENLY FATHER.

There are a number of scripture passages which give us assurance of God's parenthood to us but I especially favor this one, "He is like a father to us, tender, sympathetic to those who reverence Him." (Psalm 103:13, TLB)

BECAUSE GOD LOVES YOU AND
WANTS WHAT IS BEST FOR YOU
HE GIVES YOU ALL EIGHT
OF THESE GENEROUS LOVE GIFTS:

NO ONE IS MORE CONCERNED
ABOUT YOUR WELL BEING
THAN GOD, YOUR HEAVENLY FATHER.

1. LIFE AND OPPORTUNITY. The very first words in the Bible are "In the beginning God created the heaven and earth." (Genesis 1:1) Even before God created man He created the heavens and the earth with unlimited opportunities. Then God breathed into man the breath of life, a love breath, and said, "It's all yours!" CREATED TO EXPLORE AND MASTER THE EARTH—THAT'S YOU!

2. OUT OF LOVE—GOD GIVES US LAWS FOR OUR PROTECTION AND WELL-BEING. In one of the first books of the Bible, Deuteronomy 29:9, we are exhorted, "Be careful to do the words of this covenant, that ye may prosper in all that you do." God has never given us a law to live by that was not for the purpose of blessing us and guiding us in prosperous and happy living!

The giving of the law is God's way of saying that He wants to guide you in principles which will give you the fullest, most satisfying life possible. The first table of the law said in essence, "Love God with all your heart. Do not insult His love by serving or worshipping other gods or cursing His name. Show your love by giving one day in seven in special worship of Him." The second table essentially said this: "To have a really blessed life, in your interpersonal relations, love others as you love yourself. Begin this love at home by respect for your parents. Make sure you also have respect for human life, your neighbor's wife and property. Lying about others or desiring their possessions will not make you happy either.[1]"

GOD DOESN'T WANT YOU TO SUFFER THE DESTRUCTION FROM THE SIN OF BROKEN LAWS. Face it, law breaking is destructive, devastating, and self-defeating. Sure sin has its pleasures. To say that sin is not inviting or enticing would be to lie. It woos us, it invites us, it sells us, it waters our appetite, but when we yield we suffer the consequences. "The wages of sin is death." (Romans 6:23) "But the man who commits adultry is an utter fool, for he destroys his own soul. Wounds and constant disgrace are his lot, for the woman's husband will be furious in his jealousy, and he will have no mercy on you in the day of vengeance." (Proverbs 6:32-34, TLB) The Old Testament vividly depicts the suffering and heartbreak which King David brought into his life by breaking God's love laws. BECAUSE GOD LOVES YOU HE HAS SET UP BOUNDARIES FOR YOUR WELL-BEING.

I was sitting at one of those never-turn-green traffic signals waiting for the light to turn left. As I waited and waited the fuse on my patience had about burned down to blast off. I thought to myself, "Here I sit. All this time lost, and nothing is coming from the other direction. Why can't I just go ahead and turn anyway? Why do we have to have these

70

1. Norman L. Geisler, *The Christian Ethic of Love* (Grand Rapids, Michigan: Zondervan, 1973) p. 46.

stupid traffic lights? All they do is stop us and delay our forward motion."

Then the thought came to me, "I wonder what it would be like without traffic lights and stop signs? Wouldn't it be nice if we could just do away with all the traffic signs?" Would it? You think we have murder on the highway now. What would it be like with everyone going through intersections at their own will and at high rates of speed. You wouldn't be able to even drive down the road without getting killed for sure. You see, as much as we don't like waiting at the traffic lights, all the delays and all the stops are for our own protection and well-being. Without them it would be murder. I said "Thank you, Jesus, for this traffic signal that saves me from bodily injury and death itself."

This is exactly why God gave us the Commandments. They are our traffic signals in life to protect us. Look all around you at the crack ups, the breakdowns, all the hurting and deep emotional wounding; all the result of breaking the laws that God has laid down for our well-being. IT'S SIMPLE, OBEY THE RULES GOD HAS GIVEN US OUT OF HIS LOVE FOR US AND HAVE GOOD EMOTIONAL-MENTAL HEALTH. OR BREAK THEM AND BRING GREAT INJURY TO YOURSELF AND OTHERS.

LOVE GAVE ALL THE COMMANDMENTS
AND
LOVE FULFILLS ALL THE COMMANDMENTS

3. BECAUSE GOD LOVES US HE DISCIPLINES US TO BRING THE BEST OUT OF US.

Simply because God loves us, and passionately wants what is best for us, he disciplines and corrects us. "If you refuse to discipline your son, it proves that you don't love him. For if you love him you will be prompt to punish him." (Proverbs 13:24, TLB) MY DAD SURE DID LOVE ME! He must have because when I was a boy growing up, when I got too big for my pants, he warmed the seat of them! When I was feeling the sting I never could figure out why he said it hurt him more than it hurt me. Now, since I have become a father, I understand.

GOD'S KIND OF LOVE IS NOT THE SOFT-SOAP KIND PEDDLED IN SO MANY CIRCLES TODAY. TRUE FATHERLY LOVE INVOLVES DISCIPLINE. "My son, don't be angry when the Lord punishes you, don't be discouraged when He has to show you where you are wrong. For when He punishes you, it proves that He loves you; when He whips you, it proves you are really His child." (Hebrews 12:5-6, TLB) God's love demands and brings the best out of His children.

4. OUT OF LOVE GOD GIVES YOU WORK TO DO FOR YOUR LIVELIHOOD, PERSONAL ACHIEVEMENT, AND PROSPERITY. Different from most government operated welfare programs, WORK is a very important part of God's unbeatable welfare program. This is what I read in the Bible in the book of Proverbs. It says in many different ways, NO WORK—NO EAT! You respond, "Pastor, that sounds cruel." Don't get mad at me. I didn't teach it; the book of Proverbs teaches it. Now, let me explain that I am not talking about people who are sick, or who are up in years, or who are the victims of some misfortune. If a person is

able-bodied and can work but doesn't work, the most loving thing you could do, in the long run, would be to tell them that they cannot eat. Why? Because laziness doesn't bring anything good out of a person. To put your best foot forward you have to step over the laziness. If you raise a child without ever teaching him how to work, are you showing him love? NO! If you love someone you will do what you need to do to help him become a responsible person. God does nothing for us that we can do for ourselves because He wants us to become responsible persons.

The story goes that Darwin Smith died and regained consciousness in the next world. He looked out over a vast expanse of pleasant country. After resting comfortably for awhile, in a delightful spot, he began to get a little bored. He called out, "Is there anybody here?"

An attendant, appropriately dressed in white, appeared and said gravely, "What do you want?"

"What can I have?" asked Smith. The attendant replied, "Whatever you want." "May I have something to eat?" asked Smith.

They brought him delicious dishes, even the things he liked best on earth. Smith was having a wonderful time eating, sleeping, and calling for more good things.

But presently he wanted something more. He called for games. They came in profusion. Then he called for books and read with excitement and pleasure. He called for anything that struck his fancy and received it in abundant measure. But at last the final boredom caught up with him and he shouted, "I want something to DO!" The attendant appeared and said, "I'm sorry, but that is the only thing we cannot give you here." By this time, Smith was frantic for something to do and in his terrible frustration, cried out, "I'm sick and tired of everything here; I'd rather go to hell!"

"Where do you think you are?" asked the attendant.

WHERE WOULD WE BE
WITHOUT WORK?
THANK YOU, JESUS
FOR LOVING ME ENOUGH
TO GIVE ME WORK TO DO!

5. PROBLEMS TO BUILD OUR CHARACTER. If we didn't have any problems to overcome how much growing and advancing would we do? It is the hard spots that make us stretch and reach and depend upon God. In my life that is when I grow. So many times people ask me, "Pastor, why does God allow pain, hurt, hardships, and obstacles to come into my life?" Look at it this way: If, as a parent, you were always taking all of the rough spots out of your child's life by overprotecting him, your child would not grow up to become a strong adult. Instead, he would grow up to be a "pansy" unable to cope with adult life. Into each of our lives God allows a certain amount of hardship to come for our own character development. As Romans 8:28 puts it, "For we know that all things work together for good to them that love God..."

6. HELP IN YOUR TIME OF NEED. What a loving Heavenly Father God is! When I was a student years ago in college and in seminary I

74

worked sometimes all night and in most spare hours to put myself through college and then seminary. Although my father did not tell me verbally, I know that he expected me to do everything that I could possibly do to pay my own way. But as my loving father he had the uncanny ability to know when I had done all I could do to pay my own way for my schooling. On more than one occasion he came to my rescue—just at the moment I needed it most!

WHAT IS YOUR NEED THIS MOMENT? "For God has said, 'I will never, never fail you nor forsake you.' That is why we can say without any doubt and fear, 'The Lord is my Helper and I am not afraid of anything that mere man can do to me.'" (Hebrews 13:5-6, TLB) IF GOD BE FOR US AND HE IS, WHY SHOULD WE WORRY AND FRET?

7. SOMETHING TO SHARE WITH OTHERS. A little boy had only a few loaves and fishes. With five thousand people and more without food, it seems like so little, but when he shared it the miracle happened and it multiplied and fed the multitude. Every reader has something that God has given him to share. As you share it your joy is going to multiply manyfold.

8. GOD'S GREATEST GIFT TO YOU IS JESUS. He has been sent of God to give you abundant life now and eternal life to come. (See John 10:10, 3:16.) Your well-being is dependent not upon anything other than receiving Jesus as Lord and Savior!

With Jesus you can be confident that your well-being will be taken care of in this life and in the life to come.

JESUS—MY SECURITY BLANKET!

At one of our Men's Breakfasts, a burly truck driver named Phil DeFresne, very effectively communicated this testimony. Hear it in his own words: "I did something few people ever do; I taught myself how to drive a truck and got a good job with a big outfit. You might say I was a self-made truck driver but I had a chip on my shoulder—no one was going to tell me what to do!"

"As a result of my neighbor and good friend, Jerry Schmidt, inviting us to New Hope, I fell in love with Jesus Christ and He has been changing my life ever since. About six months after becoming a Christian, after completing my haul for the day, my boss met me and dropped the hammer on me. He told me that they had received complaints from the customers about my sharp tongue and that I was rude and unfriendly. He told me that because of my bad attitude, they were demoting me in pay and status to driving the little compact truck. In the world of truckers, status is how large a truck you drive. So, now instead of having one of the largest trucks, I was given the smallest one in the line to drive.

"I was almost afraid to go home because I prided myself in providing well for my family and I was afraid of what my wife, Judy, would say. On the way home I stopped and talked with my pastor, whom I love very much. He pointed out to me some of the things that God was trying to teach me about how He wanted to change my attitude and live His life through me. There in his office that day I committed my problem to the Lord.

"I didn't sleep much that night but did a lot of walking the floor. The next day I was embarrassed to go to work and let those truckers see me but I went. I was feeling pretty low. But after about an hour out on the road, as I was driving that little compact truck, it seemed like the Lord, Himself, came into that truck and He was with me and He told me that He was going to change my attitude and I began to sing and be happy in Jesus!

"Within a few weeks some of the same customers who called in to complain were calling in to tell my boss what a nice guy I was and what a great job I was doing. God changed my attitude so much that all the people could see the new person that Christ was making out of Phil DuFresne. My boss responded by giving me the largest truck in the yard to drive and made me Truck Driver No. 2 in our large fleet." YES, LOVE CAN CHANGE THE ATTITUDE AND A BETTER ATTITUDE CAN MAKE A BETTER LIFE!!

GOD'S WELFARE PROGRAM BASED ON HIS LOVE CERTAINLY IS FOR OUR BEST. "Behold what manner of love the Father hath bestowed upon us, that we should be called the sons of God." (I John 3:1)

HIS BANNER OVER ME
IS LOVE!

Several years ago my staunch Christian mother was visiting us from the east and taught the members of our church family this chorus which has come to mean a great deal to us:

"GOD IS SO GOOD,
GOD IS SO GOOD, GOD IS SO GOOD,
HE'S SO GOOD TO ME.
I LOVE HIM SO,
I LOVE HIM SO, I LOVE HIM SO,
HE'S SO GOOD TO ME!"

Author Unknown

CHAPTER 6

Win With Love!

There are a great many marvelous gospel songs being written today, but I have yet to hear one that warms my heart more than the one I learned to sing as a boy:

"Oh, how I love Jesus,
Oh, how I love Jesus,
Because He first loved me."[1]

Jesus was asked by the Pharisees, "Which is the greatest commandment?" He gave the answer to man's greatest need in this reply, "Love

1. Frederick Whitefield, *Oh, How I Love Jesus* (Grand Rapids, Michigan: Singspiration, 1966)

the Lord your God with all your heart, soul, and mind." This is the first and greatest commandment. The second most important is similar: "Love your neighbor as much as you love yourself." (Matthew 22:37-39, TLB). PRACTICE THIS LOVE COMMANDMENT AND YOU WILL BE A WINNER! WITH LOVE— YOU WILL WIN AGAIN AND AGAIN!

What does it mean to love God with all one's heart, soul, and mind? I think that the answer to this is: Before anyone can really make this commitment of love to God he must first know how much God has loved him. How from the very beginning of time God has planned for his well-being, has desired to share His life, joy, and love with him.

NO GREATER LOVE THAN

THE LOVE JESUS GIVES TO ME!

OPEN YOUR HEART TO HOW

LOVED YOU ARE!

THE BIG MOMENT IN ALL OF HISTORY WAS THAT NIGHT WHEN GOD SENT HIS SON TO BE BORN. From the foundations or beginning of the world, God had been preparing for this event. In many ways and especially through the prophets, God had spoken of His Son coming. GOD CHOSE THE IDEAL PLACE AND THE IDEAL TIME FOR THIS MIRACLE TO HAPPEN! The Scripture let us know that when everything was right: "When the fullness of time was come, God sent forth His Son. (Galations 4:4)

RIGHT NOW, I WANT YOU TO USE YOUR IMAGINATION. GET LOOSE, OKAY? The place is Heaven. Like a coach talking to his quarterback in the last seconds before the final play—The Father, God, is talking to the Son, Jesus. What did he say? WHAT WAS THE LAST WORD GOD GAVE TO JESUS BEFORE SENDING HIM ON HIS IMPORTANT ASSIGNMENT OF LEADING US TO VICTORY?

WHAT GOD SAID TO JESUS WAS:
SO LIFE-CHANGING!
SO OVER-POWERING!
SO MOTIVATING!
SO BEAUTIFUL!

WHAT DEPARTING MESSAGE DID GOD GIVE TO JESUS TO BRING TO US? GOD SAID TO HIS SON, JESUS, "GIVE THEM ALL MY LOVE!!!"

Professor Howard Hendricks, who teaches at Dallas Seminary, gives his testimony to these words, "Memories of my childhood haunt me. My Roman Catholic mother and my agnostic father were separated before I was born. Most of my childhood was spent with my grandmother. If I look back into the dim recesses of my memory I can see a boy going from tavern to tavern in Philadelphia, picking up pretzels to eat along the way, looking for an alcoholic grandfather to see if I could slip the pay envelope out of the old man's back pocket before he shot the whole wad in the tavern.

"The fact that an unhappy boy with a miserable beginning like that not only has something going for his own life today, but also has something worth sharing with students across the country, is testimony to the fact that God loves the unlovely. Man, with the environment I grew up in, I was a little brat! BUT GOD CHANGED IT ALL!"[2]

THE LIVING BIBLE SAYS IT SO WELL, "WHEN WE WERE UTTERLY HELPLESS WITH NO MEANS OF ESCAPE, CHRIST CAME AT JUST THE RIGHT TIME AND DIED FOR US SINNERS WHO HAD NO USE FOR HIM" (Romans 5:6,TLB) THE GOOD NEWS IS THAT GOD, IN LOVE, HAS SENT JESUS, HIS SON, TO OUR RESCUE.

There is no greater love than this. "While we were yet sinners, Christ died for us."

"SUCH LOVE, SUCH LOVE,
SUCH WONDROUS LOVE,
THAT GOD SHOULD LOVE
A SINNER SUCH AS I,
HOW WONDERFUL, WONDERFUL
IS LOVE LIKE THIS!"[3]

GOD'S LOVE IS VIVIDLY ILLUSTRATED BEFORE OUR EYES IN THE EARTHLY LIFE OF JESUS.

JESUS LOVED WITHOUT DISCRIMINATION. His own people turned against Him because He ate with sinners. At Jacob's well he encountered an adulterous woman of the hated Samaritan race. Instead of snubbing her and treating her as dirt He

82

---

2. Howard Hendricks, *Say It With Love* (Wheaton, Illinois: Victor Books, 1973) p. 13.
3. Robert Harkness, *Such Love* (Kansas City, Missouri: Lillenas, Publishing, 1929 and 1957). Used by permission.

saw potential and value, and helped her to become a child of God. (see John 4) THERE IS NO SINNER OR OUTCAST OF ANY RACE THAT HE WILL NOT HELP BECOME A RESPECTABLE CHILD OF GOD—ISN'T THE LOVE OF JESUS SOMETHING WONDERFUL?!

JESUS LOVES IN SPITE OF. Jesus does not withhold His love, He gives it! He does not say, "reform, do as I say and then I will love you," but He loves us first. Jesus loves us as we are, with our strengths and with our weaknesses, with our past and with our future. Even while He was dying on the cross He still loved those who were putting Him to death saying, "Father, forgive them, for they know not what they do." (Luke 23:34) ISN'T THE LOVE OF JESUS SOMETHING WONDERFUL?

JESUS' LOVE IS A STUBBORN LOVE. You can't make God stop loving you! You may ignore Him, resist Him, insult Him, or reject Him. You may commit every sin in the book but you can't make God stop loving you! For example, the betrayer, Judas, who sold his Lord for thirty pieces of silver. All the time Jesus knew what was in Judas' heart. Yet, in tender love, He washed Judas' feet right along with the other disciples. He offered to Judas the morsel out of the common dish which was a gesture of true friendship. In the garden, at the very moment of betrayal, as Judas put the finger on Jesus, with a kiss of death, Jesus once again reached out to Judas in love. He said, "My friend, what made you come here?" There was no time while Judas was alive but that he could have turned back to God and been forgiven. ISN'T THE

LOVE OF JESUS SOMETHING WONDERFUL?!

Recently, I received a note from a young person and this is what it said "Pastor, no matter what happens in the future, no matter how many things change, I cannot get away from that stubborn love of God. That will not let me go! I will always live for Him for it is that stubborn love of His that I'm so crazy about!"

"ISN'T THE LOVE OF JESUS SOMETHING WONDERFUL! WONDERFUL!
WONDERFUL!
OH, ISN'T THE LOVE OF JESUS SOME-THING WONDERFUL!
WONDERFUL IT IS TO ME!" [4]

LOVE SO AMAZING, SO DIVINE,

*LOVE SO AMAZING, SO DIVINE,
DEMANDS MY LOVE, MY LIFE, MY ALL!*

BECAUSE GOD TRULY LOVES YOU, HE GIVES YOU THE DECISION TO MAKE. HIS LOVE DEMANDS RESPONSE BUT HE WILL NOT FORCE HIS LOVE UPON YOU. It is something that you must accept or reject for yourself. God will try everything to win you to Himself but if you persistently say "no," He will ultimately have to say, "Alright, have it your own way." This is your greatest decision. No one can make this decision for you. YOU CANNOT COP OUT! YOU, AND YOU ALONE, CAN MAKE THAT DECISION!

I OFFER TO YOU JESUS CHRIST. RECEIVE

4. John Peterson, *Isn't The Love Of Jesus Something Wonderful* (Grand Rapids, Michigan: Singspiration, 1961).

HIM AND YOU WILL HAVE THE GREATEST LOVE IN ALL OF THE WORLD!! Dr. Glasser wrote *Reality Therapy.* In it he says, "Every man needs one essential friend." A man or woman who has one friend with whom they can share deeply has a priceless treasure! Where can you find a friend with whom you can share your deepest dreams and disappointments, a friend you can trust to keep your confidence? I have such a friend. His name is Jesus Christ. I can go to Him and confess all my sins and know that He will put His arm around my shoulder and love me anyway. WHAT A FRIEND WE HAVE IN JESUS!

JESUS MUST BE LORD OF ALL OR HE WON'T BE YOUR LORD AT ALL. So quickly, men forget and slip back into their old ways. After the crucifixion of Jesus was out of sight, it wasn't many days until Peter and the other disciples were back fishing and living as they had before. They had forgotten what Jesus called them to do. Suddenly, Jesus appeared to them on the lake, drew them ashore, and spoke these penetrating words to Peter, "Simon, son of Jonas, lovest thou me more than these." (John 21:15) Do you love me enough to follow me when everything goes wrong? What about your love? How deep is your commitment to Jesus Christ?

WHAT JESUS WANTS TO KNOW IS HOW MUCH DO YOU LOVE HIM THIS VERY MOMENT? DO YOU LOVE HIM MORE THAN:
>   WANTING WHAT YOU WANT?
>   MONEY—AND POSSESSIONS?
>   WORLDLY PLEASURES?

JESUS HAS PROVEN HIS LOVE FOR YOU—
NOW YOU CAN RESPOND BY SHOWING HIM
YOUR LOVE:

RECEIVE JESUS AS LORD AND SAVIOR.
GIVE HIM FIRST PLACE IN YOUR
AFFECTIONS.
KEEP HIS COMMANDMENTS.
LOVE ONE ANOTHER.

LOVE AND ACCEPT YOURSELF AS A
PERSON OF VALUE AND WORTH.
TRUST GOD IN YOUR DAILY LIVING.

EXPRESS YOUR LOVE TO JESUS RIGHT NOW:

"My Jesus, I love Thee,
I know Thou art mine,
For Thee all the follies
Of sin I resign."

William R. Featherston

WITH JESUS AND HIS LOVE—
YOU WILL BE A REAL WINNER!

JESUS' LOVE IS THE MOST POSITIVE
FORCE UPON ALL THE EARTH. This love
changes everything. As Bob Benson says:

"It makes heavy burdens light,
Long hours short,
Ordinary faces beautiful,
Houses into homes,
Picnics into banquets,
Wilted daisies into bouquets,
God into sacrifice,
Sinners into saints." [5]

The absence of love is the real explanation of the unhappiness and restlessness of people today. The kind of love that comes from knowing Jesus Christ and fellowshipping with Him is the one thing that will make life good when everything else goes bad. When a person has Jesus and His love, his life is good—no matter what else he may or may not have. But without love life is one bad scene!

No doubt, you have heard of one of America's greatest ministers, Norman Vincent Peale. Did you know that along side of this successful man stands his companion, his wife, Ruth Peale? She is a tremendous author in her own right. In her book, *Adventures Of Being A Wife*, she relates this love story:

"Jack Kyle was Chief Engineer of the New York Authority. One thousand engineers and technicians worked under him. Name almost any of the great engineering projects in New York City—the Lincoln Tunnel, the lower level of the George Washington Bridge, Kennedy, LaGuardia and Newark Airports, the beginning of the World Trade Center—all of these were built under Jack's genius and guidance.

"He and his wife were about as close as it is possible for a couple to be. Virginia was a gentle, very beautiful, highly intelligent woman. It was a

5. Bob Benson, *Come Share The Being* (Nashville, Tennessee: Impact Books, 1974) p. 58.

terrible blow to all of us when she was stricken with cancer. The doctors said that nothing could be done; that it was just a matter of time.

"Jack Kyle accepted the verdict with quiet resignation. 'I don't know how I'll live without her,' he said to Norman. 'But we've had a wonderful life together. I'm grateful for that. If it's God's will that Virginia go first then His will be done.'

"In the hospital, Virginia's condition steadily worsened. Her husband spent hours at her bedside. Then suddenly, with no warning, a heart attack struck Jack. He lingered a few days. Then came a second attack and he was dead.

"It was impossible to keep the truth from his wife; when her husband did not come to see her. She guessed—and no one had the heart to hide the sad fact from her. She asked quietly when the funeral was to be. When told that it was to be Sunday at the Marble Collegiate Church, at two-thirty, she said that she was going to be there. In her condition the doctor said that was impossible. But she would not accept this. She kept saying that she was going to be there.

"One-half hour before the funeral, Virginia Kyle died. And when Norman conducted the service for her husband no one in the church had any doubts. Virginia had said she would be there. And she was."[6]

YOU CAN'T BEAT THE KIND OF LOVE THAT COMES FROM KNOWING AND WALKING WITH JESUS. IT WINS AGAIN AND AGAIN. IT WINS IN LIFE AND IN DEATH. BE A WINNER—FALL IN LOVE WITH JESUS.

6. Ruth Peale, *Adventures Of Being A Wife* (Englewood, Cliff, New Jersey: Prentice-Hall, 1971) p. 265-266.

I OFFER TO YOU JESUS CHRIST
RECEIVE HIM AS YOUR LORD
AND YOU WILL HAVE
WINNING LOVE!

CHAPTER 7

Love Is Like A Magic Penny

THERE ARE SOME REALLY NEAT THINGS
GOD HAS BEEN TEACHING ME ABOUT LOVE.
I tell you, learning how to love God's way is the
most venturesome and stimulating trip I have ever
taken! The beauty, the splendor, and the heights of
God's kind of love are absolutely breathtaking!
Travel the earth and you will find no earthly
substitute that could hold a candle to the warm,
eternal light of God's brilliant love.

GOD'S LOVE IS TO OUR SOULS WHAT THE
SUN IS TO OUR EARTH. Can you imagine what
would happen to our earth without the sun? There

would be no light, so we would be in darkness. There would be no warmth, so everything would turn to ice, wither, die, and perish. Experts tell us that a person can survive three weeks without food and three days without water, but without warmth he could not be expected to last for more than three hours. Without the warmth from the sun every living thing beginning with man would shiver, shrivel, and soon die. So it is without God's love: Man struggles, withers, and perishes without hope. BUT WITH LOVE, AS WITH THE SUN, EVERYTHING BLOOMS WITH BEAUTY! EVERYTHING LIGHTS UP WITH LIFE! No wonder the scripture declares—LOVE IS THE GREATEST! (I Corinthians 13:13)

"Where do I find love?" the middle-aged divorcee asked me. She told me that her mother didn't want her and her stepfather had beaten her until she ran away from home as a teenager, never to return. She had been through several marriages and still hadn't found love. She said, "I don't trust anyone and no one is going to get close to me." My heart went out to her, because I could see that she was a hurting person, and I observed that she was preoccupied with herself. As a result, she was withdrawing more and more from other people. Everyone wants to be loved and yet the strange thing is that so many people keep moving away from love, instead of towards it. You see, preoccupation with self is the enemy to love.

In the spirit of Christ's love, I said to this dear lady, "Your preoccupation with yourself has become a brick wall four feet thick that shuts out other people and love from your life." Then I said, "Before you'll ever receive love you have got to get out of your self-made shell and give love to other people." Somewhat taken back by my frankness, yet interested in being helped, she managed to mumble the words, "How do I do that?" I told her, "Jesus said that if we lose our life, we will find it." You see, if you totally give your old selfish self to Jesus Christ He will make you a brand new person. Then as you become interested in other people and give your concern and love to them I guarantee you that you are going to discover love. For the sound psychological spiritual principle is that it is in giving love that we receive, "For whatsoever a man sows, that he also reaps." (Galatians 6:7).

GIVING LOVE WORKS WONDERS

YES, WE ALL HAVE AN ENORMOUS NEED TO BE LOVED—BUT FAR GREATER THAN OUR NEED TO BE LOVED IS OUR NEED TO GIVE LOVE. When God created you he gave you the ability to choose to give love to others. But if you choose to withhold your love; to sit around and feel sorry for yourself; wishing that others would love you first; you are going to live without love. You see, your happiness and fulfillment depend upon your entering into the lives of those around you and giving your love away. GIVING LOVE TO OTHERS IS THE MOST IMPORTANT THING THAT YOU HAVE TO DO!

BEFORE YOU CAN REAP
A HARVEST OF LOVE
YOU MUST FIRST SOW THE
SEEDS OF LOVE!

GIVING LOVE
WILL MAKE YOU LOVABLE!

One morning a Christian friend dropped by my office to chat. After we talked for a few minutes he smiled and said, "I thank God for you, Pastor." Then as he got up to leave he put the icing on the cake by saying, "I love you." All day long I appreciated his expression of love very much. As I thought about it I said to myself, "Now there is what I call a lovable person."

MY PRAYER: "GOD, HELP ME TO BE MORE LOVABLE..." Sometimes I have trouble being lovable to people who I think are going to try and sell me something. I have an extra strong sales resistance. "God, help me to be wise in what I buy but still to be more lovable to sales persons." Now before you start thinking that I am the only person who needs to be more lovable, how about you? What about your actions and attitude towards other people, with whom you come into business contact? What is the first impression you make on another person?

Do you
    smile or frown?
Are you
    friendly or aloof?
Do you make it
    easy or hard
        for people to like you?

I THINK WE, AS CHRISTIANS, SHOULD BE THE MOST LOVABLE PEOPLE IN THE WORLD!

Right after my wife and I were married we moved into our first house. Being very proud of our new home, and wanting it to be fixed up just right, we had a salesman come out to assist us in selecting some very attractive custom-made draperies. The salesman told us it would take six weeks to make the drapes. We thought that was a long time but we would have to wait. The sixth week came, and the seventh week, and the eighth week, and the ninth week ... still no drapes. Four months after the date we were promised delivery on our drapes we still had bare sheets hanging on the windows.

I had HAD IT! I called the store and gave the woman, whose job it was to take calls, a piece of my mind. As I hung up the phone, having unloaded on an innocent woman, who had nothing to do with the delay, the words of Jesus came ringing in my ears, "In as much as you did it to the least of these, my brethren, you did it unto me." You see, two wrongs never make a right! The company had been wrong in not fulfilling their promise but I was very much in the wrong in treating this innocent lady as the enemy. Let's face it—I had not been a lovable person. I WANT TO BE A LOVABLE PERSON—DON'T YOU??

NEXT TIME, WHEN YOU ARE TEMPTED TO BE NASTY TO ANOTHER INDIVIDUAL, AND

YOU WILL BE—STOP!! THINK WHAT YOU ARE ABOUT TO DO! Are you treating that person as you want to be treated? The Bible penetrates into our very being when it says, "But if a person isn't loving and kind, it shows that he doesn't know God—for God is love." (I John 4:8, TLB). You see—"Love is very patient and kind." (I Corinthians 13:4, TLB)

A LITTLE KINDNESS WORKS WONDERS. As Christians this is the exciting way we are to live. "Stop being mean, bad-tempered, and angry. Quarreling, harsh words, and dislike of others should have no place in your lives. Instead, be kind to each other, tender-hearted, forgiving one another, just as God has forgiven you because you belong to Christ." (Ephesians 4:31, 32, TLB). YOU WANT TO BE A PERSON WHOM OTHERS LOVE?

IT IS SIMPLE—
BE KIND!
AND YOU'LL BE
A LOVABLE PERSON!

LOVE SEES THE BEST!

When Jesus Christ comes into your life, and His Spirit has His right-of-way within you, you will become a loving optimist. Negative, pessimistic attitudes do not come from the Spirit of God!

Returning to my office one evening, after being in Seattle to do the Seattle Today Show on Channel 5, I found this message on my desk, left by my secretary, Carol: "A woman called to compliment you on your sermon about Love. She is excited about New Hope and her husband likes it, too. She has discussed the sermon with her daughter and they are helping her to overcome a personal problem."

Carol arrived at the office on Wednesday morning and I told her that I had enjoyed reading the note from this lady, who is a newcomer to New Hope. Carol added that the woman had great enthusiasm in her voice as she talked about New Hope over the phone. She told Carol that last Sunday, as she was enjoying our scenic outside drive-in service, she looked up at the giant white screen that towers over the platform and there were birds all lined up on the top of the screen in a row. In the true spirit of an optimist she commented that it appeared that even the birds enjoyed hearing the Pastor preach. Upon hearing this I told Carol that someone else, upon observing the same birds sitting lined up atop the screen might make this observation, "Pastor Galloway's sermons are for the birds!" What a difference it makes in how we look at something. You are going to find what you look for.

LOVE ALWAYS FINDS THE BEST— BECAUSE LOVE LOOKS FOR THE BEST!

Robert Young, a Presbyterian pastor, told this story in one of his sermons: "One day a minister came in to see me, and he was depressed. He said, 'I had a funeral yesterday for a beautiful Christian woman.' I asked him, 'Well, why has that got you

down? We have funerals all of the time!' The
minister said, 'Frankly, it was the way I treated the
woman who died. I came to my church, looked
across the membership roll, and noticed the name of
a woman whom I had never met. Someone told me,
she used to be such a faithful worker and was a
beautiful Christian woman, but then something
happened. She stopped coming to church about
three years ago, and boy, has she changed! She
won't have anything to do with anyone anymore.
She is such a snobbish, secretive person! We think
it's because she inherited some money. Those who
have stopped over to the house say that she's
always lounging around in very expensive, flimsy
negligees, wearing expensive perfume, and a glass
of liquor is always within reach. She watches
television constantly and what's worse, once a week
when her husband is at work, a strange man with an
out-of-town license plate drives up, goes in, and
stays about an hour and leaves! Pity the way a good
Christian can suddenly go to the devil.'

   " 'Then suddenly one day she died,' the minister
recalled, 'and her husband came to me and asked if I
would conduct the service for her. I told him that I
would but that I thought that she was no longer a
member of the church. I told him what I knew about
her. The husband was shocked!' 'My wife,' he
explained, 'had an incurable, fatal disease that hit
her three years ago! She bought this perfume to
cover the odor and she only wore flimsy negligees so
that the weight of clothing would not hurt her
abdomen. The liquor was a bonafide medicine. The
man coming to see her once a week was a specialist

from out of town. She was secretive because she wanted to keep it from the kids, so they wouldn't know they were going to lose their mom. Oh, she was a beautiful Christian all through it, to the end!' "

A minister friend of mine lived in constant frustration with his people. He was plagued with a severe allergy, ulcers, and migraine headaches. The pastor was released when he followed the suggestion of a spiritual leader who said, "Why don't you get off the judgment seat and get on the mercy seat?" To live on the judgment seat is to become a miserable critic, condemning and separating yourself from others. To live on the mercy seat is to overlook, forgive, give the benefit of the doubt, and go the second mile. Enjoy fellowship with others!

If you really love someone you are willing to overlook a lot of things. "Love does not keep a record of wrongs." We call it hurt feelings, righteous indignation, or something else but what we really mean is our love curdles when it is offended. Quarrels, tension, coldness in a relationship often come as a result of our wanting to cherish grievances. NO HUMAN RELATIONSHIP CAN ENDURE FOR LONG WITHOUT A GREAT DEAL OF FORBEARANCE AND MAKING ALLOWANCES.

GIVE YOURSELF A BIG LOVE-LIFT. MAKE IT A HABIT TO LOOK FOR THE BEST IN OTHERS. You'll never go wrong by giving others the benefit of the doubt. A lot of people look for the worst and they create a negative atmosphere all around them. In the spirit of magnanimous love train yourself to believe the best first, second, and always—until facts are produced to show you differently. Then, look at the facts, protect yourself from being hurt if you need to and then go ahead and overlook the faults and love the person anyway.

ACCORDING TO THE BIBLE LOVE ALWAYS BELIEVES THE BEST. "If you love someone, you will be loyal to him no matter what the cost. You will always believe in him, always expect the best of him, and always stand your ground in defending him." (ICorinthians 13:7, TLB).

LOVE IS NOT UNREALISTIC. IT SEES WHAT IS WRONG WITH ANOTHER PERSON—BUT IT CHOOSES ALSO TO SEE THE BEST. When Jesus looks at you, He doesn't just see your ugly sins, shortcomings, and faults. He sees the good in you. He sees what you can become, with His help. Michelangelo, when he looked at the rough chunk of castoff marble, exclaimed, "I see an angel." Then he set to work to chisel and carve with tender care until out of an ugly rough piece of marble came a beautiful angel that has inspired millions. BELIEVE THE BEST IN OTHERS AND YOU WILL BRING THE BEST OUT OF THEM. THERE ARE PEOPLE, WHOSE LIVES YOU TOUCH THIS DAY, WHO DESPERATELY NEED YOU TO SEE THEM THROUGH THE EYES OF LOVE.

Remember what Goethe said:
"TREAT PEOPLE AS IF THEY WERE
WHAT THEY OUGHT TO BE
AND
YOU HELP THEM TO BECOME
WHAT THEY ARE CAPABLE OF BEING."

WHAT BEAUTY BLOOMS—FROM
SEEING
AND
BEING SEEN
THROUGH THE EYES OF LOVE
LOVE IS LIKE A MAGIC PENNY—
WHEN YOU GIVE IT AWAY.

While pastoring my first church in Columbus, Ohio, I stepped into the kindergarten class one Sunday to observe and I learned an unforgettable lesson from them. You know, it's amazing what we adults can learn from children. After all these years, I can still see the happy faces of those four and five year olds as they were singing in their high-pitched little voices, these words:

"LOVE IS SOMETHING, IF YOU GIVE IT AWAY, GIVE IT AWAY, IT'S JUST LIKE A MAGIC PENNY, IF YOU GIVE IT AWAY, YOU END UP HAVING MORE."

WHAT YOU GIVE—IS WHAT YOU GET. In a sermon, entitled Manage Your Moods, Dr. Robert Schuller tells this anecdote: "Once there was a little boy who was strongly admonished and rebuked by his mother. In a moment of anger, he yelled at her and said, "I hate you!" Then he heard a voice (his echo) coming back to him, a stranger out of the woods saying, "I hate you! I hate you! I hate you!" That scared him. He ran back to his mother and said, "Mother, there is a mean man in the woods. He's out there calling, and saying, "I hate you! I hate you! I hate you!" His mother said, "Just a minute, son." She took him back to the hill and she said, "Shout as loud as you can into the woods, 'I love you! I love you! I love you!'" So he did, "I love you! I love you! I love you!'" So he did, "I love you! I love you! I love you!" "So it is in life," his mother said, "Life treats you the way you treat life. Life is an echo."[1]

LOVE LIFE AND IT WILL LOVE YOU BACK.
LOVE OTHERS AND THEY WILL
LOVE YOU BACK!

"But, how do you give love?" a lonely man in his late forties asked me. "My friend," I answered, "Here are some ways in which you can give love:"
By Being With
By Accepting
By Caring
By Listening
By Helping
By Gifts
By Believing In
By Edifying

1. Robert Schuller, Sermon, *Manage Your Moods*, © by Robert Schuller, Garden Grove Community Church.

and
Most of all by being a
Channel for God's Love
to flow through you!

Ann Kiemel is a young Dean of Women on a Christian college campus near Boston, Massachusetts. Just about every weekend she travels across the country, taking the love of Jesus everywhere she goes. In her book, "I'm Out To Change My World," she tells the story about a taxi driver in Miami with whom she shared God's love: "It was in the summer, and I got into a beat-up old cab in Miami Beach, and asked the old cab driver to take me to another hotel. It was hot and every window was rolled down.

"I asked him, 'What is the one word that describes your life?' He answered, 'Can I give you two?' He was old and gnarled, about as beat up as his cab. 'Yes' I said, 'What are they?' He replied, 'Bored and unhappy.'

" 'Sir, why are those the two words that describe your life?' And he said, 'I don't know. I guess 'cause I got nobody in the world.' I said, 'Nobody, Sir? No wife, no children, no family? No one in the whole world for you?' He just said, 'No.'

"I said, 'Tell me, Sir, how did you get to be an old man and have nobody?' He sighed, 'Cause I never got a good job, and no woman wanted me.' 'Sir, can I sing you a song?'

"He looked at me, 'Sing?' I said, 'I don't have a very good voice, but I know you'd like my song.'

"He said, 'Just a minute, please' and he rolled up his window, and then nodded at me.

"And I began to sing:

Something beautiful
Something good
All my confusion,
He understood!
All I had to offer Him
Was brokenness and strife.
But He's making something beautiful
Out of my life! [2]

" 'Sir, do you know who I'm singing about? Jesus Christ! He's the Lord of my life. He'll laugh with you. He'll be your friend.' And just then, we pulled under the portico of the next hotel, and I was fumbling in my purse for my money, when I saw this old hand reach out and I let loose of the money in my purse. I reached out and took his hand—almost afraid to look him in the eye, because I didn't know what he would say. I lifted my eyes to his, and he was crying.

" 'Lady, when I got in this cab tonight, I was the loneliest person in the whole world. I never heard anyone talk like you have talked tonight, and I want your God. He and I could ride together.'

"And I crawled out of that cab knowing that somewhere in Miami Beach, an old, gnarled, wrinkled man drives a beat-up old cab. But he doesn't drive it alone. And I can hardly help but sing when I know that the eternal God is willing to invade an old cabbie's life, and love him." [3]

---

2. *Something Beautiful*. Copyright © 1971 by William J. Gaither. International copyright secured. Used by permission. Composed by Bill and Gloria Gaither.

3. Ann Kiemel, *I'm Out To Change My World* (Nashville, Tennessee: Impact Books, 1974) p. 17-19.

ANN HAS A LOT OF LOVE TO GIVE. AND YOU, TOO, HAVE A LOT OF LOVE TO GIVE. REMEMBER—

"LOVE IS SOMETHING, IF YOU GIVE IT AWAY, GIVE IT AWAY, IT'S JUST LIKE A MAGIC PENNY, IF YOU GIVE IT AWAY, YOU END UP HAVING MORE!

CHAPTER 8

Love Begins At Home

A father and mother finally had one of those rare nights out, away from the children, just the two of them. As they were driving along in silence, and the full moon was shining, warm feelings of romance began to find their way to the surface in Joyce. From the other side of the front seat, she said, "James, do you remember how, before we were married you used to snuggle up real close to me in the car everytime we went someplace?" James replied, "You know it is the strangest thing—I'm still sitting in the same spot." IF YOU DON'T FEEL CLOSE TO YOUR MATE, MAYBE YOU

SHOULD STOP AND ASK YOURSELF, "WHO HAS MOVED?"

After Johnny had attended Sunday School for three consecutive Sundays he was asked by his teacher, "Johnny, would you like to go to Heaven someday?" In complete honesty, Johnny said, "I'm not sure. I don't know what Heaven is like." The teacher thought that she had better think of something quick, so she explained, "Johnny, Heaven is kind of like home." Without hesitation, Johnny said, "No way am I going there, if it is like my home." WHAT DO YOUR CHILDREN FEEL ABOUT THEIR HOME? IS IT A HEAVENLY PLACE OR IS IT THE OPPOSITE OR POSSIBLY SOMEWHERE BETWEEN? WHERE LOVE IS, IT IS ALWAYS A BIT OF HEAVEN!

*WHAT WE ARE AT HOME
IS WHERE WE ARE WITH GOD.*

Without a doubt, the two most important questions in a child's life are, "Daddy and Mommy, do you love me? Daddy and Mommy, do you love each other?" If the answer is yes, all is well. If not, nothing else will make up for the missing love.

Out of love and concern for you and your children Jesus said, "And so I am giving a new commandment to you now—love each other just as much as I love you." (John 13:34, TLB).

What I am about to say now is one of the most important truths that you could ever read:

LOVE
BEGINS
AT
HOME!

LOVE IS THE ONLY WAY
TO RAISE A CHILD

LOVE ENOUGH TO DISCIPLINE . . "If you refuse to discipline your son, it proves that you don't love him." (Proverbs 13:24, TLB). Yes, your child needs discipline, but discipline alone is not enough. "I can remember how my dad, being a church administrator, had to travel alot and mother used to get after us boys. She would take me off into the bedroom and talk to me. On more than one occasion, she would administer a switching to my backside to make her point that I needed to improve my behavior. The thing that I can remember most is that she never disciplined me without giving me her love. Love was the priceless gift that my mother always gave to me." ALWAYS DISCIPLINE OUT OF LOVE AND NEVER OUT OF ANGER.

HOW CAN YOU TEACH SELF-DISCIPLINE
IF YOU ARE OUT OF CONTROL YOURSELF?

CONTROL YOUR CHILD'S BEHAVIOR
WITH LOVE!

TEACH IN LOVE. I have become increasingly aware that as parents, God has given us the responsibility to be teachers. Let me ask you a question. How will your child learn responsibility, respect, and God's spiritual principles for successful living, unless by both word and action you teach him? This faithful promise is yours: "Train a child up in the way he should go; and when he is old, he will not depart from it." (Proverbs 22:6). STOP AND THINK—WHAT ARE YOU TEACHING YOUR CHILD? ARE YOU TEACHING HIM WHAT YOU WANT HIM TO LEARN OR IS HE LEARNING SOME THINGS FROM YOU THAT YOU WISH HE WASN'T LEARNING?

Eight days of being away from our 20 month old daughter, Ann, was a pretty long time, and boy, were we glad to see her upon our return home! Although Ann had beautiful, loving care while we were gone, she was so excited to see her Daddy and Mommy!

Our first morning home, while I was in the bathroom shaving, Ann came in to join me—which I thought was pretty super! The only catch was that she brought her whole can of blocks along, and proceeded to turn them upside down and dump them all over my feet. Well, I was so overjoyed to be home with her that I didn't even mind standing in the middle of her blocks while I was shaving.

As I finished shaving, I noticed that she had finished playing, so I told her to pick up the blocks and return them inside the can to her room. A few minutes later, I came back to supervise the job, and found that she had put about half of the blocks in the can and taken them to her room. Now, if Ann had been six years old, I would have disciplined her for not completing the job, but since she is 20 months old, and a 20 month old attention span is not very long, I concluded that she had done exceptionally well.

However, I wanted her to learn to complete a job. So, in order to teach her, I took her by the hand and led her back into the bathroom. Daddy and Ann got down on the bathroom floor together and finished picking up the blocks and putting them in the can. Once finished, I put the lid on the can and handed it to Ann. Happy as a lark, she toddled off to her room and placed the blocks on her shelf. TAKE ADVANTAGE OF EVERY OPPORTUNITY THAT IS YOURS TO TEACH YOUR CHILD IN LOVE. IT IS ABSOLUTELY AMAZING WHAT GOOD THINGS CHILDREN LEARN WHEN THEY ARE TAUGHT IN LOVE!

EXERCISE LOVE TO BUILD SELF-ESTEEM IN YOUR CHILDREN. At a Christian Women's gathering, the admirable helpmate of one of America's well known Christian leaders, shared this from her heart. They had little or no trouble from any of their children, until last year when one of the younger girls started Junior High School. To their alarm, the girl became very negative and even rebellious towards her parents. As the girl's wise father and perceptive mother talked it over with God in prayer, the insight came from God to them that this daughter needed more reassurance of their love. DON'T YOU EVER FORGET IT—TEEN-AGERS NEVER GET TOO OLD TO NEED LOVE—THEY JUST NEED MORE!

The mother took positive action by making a

point to go into the daughter's room each morning and spend time with her, expressing love and telling the girl how beautiful she was becoming, and gently stroking the girl's hair. She put her arm around her and held her close, letting her know without any doubt that she was a very special and loved girl. Listen to this, within one week all the rebellion and all the negativeness was gone!

LOVE
WINS
AGAIN
AND
AGAIN!

PRAISE
IS THE GREATEST HOME EXERCISE
YOU CAN DO.
HOW IS YOUR EXERCISE PROGRAM?

Dr. Charles Allen in his book, *The Miracle of Love,* shared this experience. "I talked to a mother just recently, whose teenage daughter is in trouble. She is not married, and she is going to have a baby. The mother said many harsh and bitter things about her. She talked about their family being disgraced. I finally said to that mother, 'Stop saying all those bitter things. That girl is hurt enough. You go home and tell that girl, and keep telling her many times everyday, that you love her, and that you are standing by her, that you are going to help her all the way through.' I told that mother, 'If you do not love your daughter now, she will likely never need your love again.'"

When Jesus wanted people to understand what God is like, He told them about a father who welcomed his prodigal son back home. Instead of fussing at the boy, the father "fell on his neck and kissed him." (Luke 15:20).[1] GOD, HELP US TO LOVE OUR CHILDREN IN THE SAME UN-STOPPABLE WAY YOU LOVE US!

> *"CHILDREN NEED LOVE,*
> *ESPECIALLY WHEN THEY*
> *DO NOT DESERVE IT."*
>
> Harold S. Hulbert

TAKE TIME TO LOVE.

Publisher, Bob Benson, who is the kind of dad that every boy should have, shared this experience of his own relationship with his son. "One night I bent over and kissed Patrick and quickly stood up and started out of the room. I was so tired it was about the last 'get up' that I had left for the whole day, I thought. Then he stopped me cold, and brought me back to his bedside, and asked, 'Why do you kiss me so fast?'"

This question made Bob ask himself, "And why do we let the finest, most precious moments of our

1. Charles L. Allen, *The Miracle of Love* (Old Tappan, New Jersey: Fleming H. Revell Co., 1972)

lives go by without a word, thinking that tomorrow on our vacation there will be time to hike, swim, and love our children? Why do we withhold from them the very thing they need the most—ourselves and our love?" [2]

THERE WAS A TIME IN MY LIFE WHEN I DIDN'T TAKE THE TIME TO LOVE THOSE CLOSEST TO ME AND THE RESULTS WERE TRAGIC AND DEVASTATING. In 1970, I wrote these words in a sermon, "How many hours I worked in a week no one knew, because I never stopped to count them. I had peeled everything else off my life, except the carrying out of my mission. As a pastor, I had become unbalanced in my living and in my relationship with those dearest and closest to me. God has shown me that I need to change my life-style, that I need to have more balance in my life. I need to take time to love." A few days later, after writing this confession, my wife divorced me. I had awakened to the truth that I needed to take time to love too late.

Out of a most disastrous experience God has taught me the essential lesson of taking time to love. Just this past Wednesday night I had six different things that I could have done. Demanding things, urgent things, good things for Jesus, but none as far-reaching as taking the time to love and spend the evening at home with my family. After all these years, I am finally learning to live with some undone work. Thank you, Jesus!

My daily goal is set by Paul in I Corinthians, when he admonishes us to: "LET LOVE BE YOUR

2. Bob Benson, *Come Share The Being* (Nashville, Tennessee: Impact Books, 1975) p. 98.

GREATEST AIM." (I Corinthians 14:1, TLB).

THE TIME TO TELL YOUR FAMILY
YOU LOVE THEM IS—NOW—BEFORE:
   ---They grow up and leave
   ---They get into trouble
   ---They turn away from you
   ---They look somewhere else for love

BEFORE

TIME HAS PASSED AWAY
AND
IT'S TOO LATE!

My friend, and well known author, Joyce Landorf, shares this story in her book, *Mourning Song:* "I remember an old man at Los Angeles International Airport who broke my heart over his regrets. We were both waiting to board a jet to Hawaii. I was on my way overseas to do a speaking and singing tour for the United States Army Chaplains. The man was just sitting beside me when, out of the corner of my eye, I noticed that he was very silently sitting there crying. I was about to ask him if I could help, when a man on the other side of him did it for me.

"The old man just shook his head 'no' and continued to cry. When he got a firmer grip on himself, he began talking—not to anyone in particular, but out loud as to why he was on his way to Hawaii. He told about his wife nagging him for thirty years about taking a Hawaiian vacation. Twenty years ago, when they had become financially able to afford such a trip, she really nagged him. He had firmly said, 'No' and given her his reasons. After all, Hawaii held no interest for him, and he couldn't see any point in going all that way and paying all that money to see an island or two.

"Then he said,'Six months ago she got cancer and now—now, she's gone.' His tears were streaming down his face, but he made no move to dry them. He just continued, 'Before she died, she made me promise I'd go and take that vacation in Hawaii for her—so here I am alone—going to Hawaii. God, why didn't I take her when we had all that time and all those years?' " [3]

"LIFE IS LIKE A VAPOR, IT
APPEARETH FOR A LITTLE WHILE, THEN
VANISHETH AWAY."

(James 4:14, TLB)

LOVE SOMEHOW FINDS THE TIME. Ray was a busy teenager. He was President of the Student Body, President of the Hi Y Club, football player in football season, basketball player in basketball season, in the class play, very active in his church, and working as a carry out boy in a supermarket on Saturdays to earn extra money. He didn't have

114

3. Joyce Landorf, *Mourning Song* (Old Tappan, New Jersey: Fleming H. Revell Co., 1974) p. 96.

time or energy to spare. But when Nancy started to his school she caught his eye. Soon he was standing in the hallway at school, hoping she might pass by and give him a smile. He soon found time to talk to her on the phone and to make the time to take her out on dates. How did he find all of this extra time? Where did all of this extra bounding energy suddenly come from? LOVE ALWAYS FINDS A WAY—YES, LOVE WILL BRING US TOGETHER!

THERE IS NO EXCUSE
ACCEPTABLE
FOR NOT LOVING—NOW!

MAKE MEALTIME A HAPPY TIME OF SHARING. Don't permit anything negative or anything that has to do with correcting be done at the dinner table. One young lady told me that she had ulcers in her stomach because when she was being brought up, all the scolding was done at the dinner table. MAKE MEALTIME A HAPPY TIME OF SHARING AND CONVERSING TOGETHER IN LOVE.

LOVE WILL BRING US TOGETHER
LOVE IS THE OPPOSITE OF BEING:
    ALONE
    APART
    SEPARATED
    SHUT OUT
LOVE WILL BRING US TOGETHER!

There is so much that God wants to teach us about His more excellent way of love. With a touch of God, love can revive and live again.

There are some of you who have thought it was too late. That's the way it is and that's the way it will always be. I say, not so! The same God of love who brought Jesus forth from the dead specializes in resurrecting dead marriages. No matter how dead the marriage is, when two imperfect mates commit themselves to begin to love God's way, the marriage will come alive with a new and greater love.

Just this week a salesman came into my office, and during the conversation he shared with me how two years ago the love in his marriage was dead. He and his wife had both killed it by insisting on their own way. With joy in his eye, he told me that in recent months, since he had started loving his wife the way God told him to in the Bible, she was responding back and loving him. For them, love had come alive and now they were living and growing together in love. A dull, sad relationship had been turned into an exciting happy marriage. GOD'S LOVE CAN MAKE THE DIFFERENCE IN YOUR HOME!

LOVE GROWS WHEN WE WORK AT IT. Falling in love is easy, but staying in love has to be worked at! It is more than just staying in love. As we work at it, it grows and expands and enlarges and becomes more beautiful. Many people never know the true abundance of love because they stop working long before the harvest comes in.

I enjoy the old story about the man who had what

many would say was a rather peculiar habit. For years he had a special date with his wife every Friday night. He would come home in the afternoon, shave and shower, put on his best clothes, go outside, walk around the block, come back and ring the doorbell. His wife would greet him at the door. They would go sit for a few minutes in the living room and talk and then they would go out for dinner together. Later in the evening, they would drive up in front of the house. He would escort her to the door, put the car in the garage, and come in through the back door. Maybe this sounds a little silly to some of you men to do something like this with your wife, but let me tell you that when this man died, his wife watered his grave with tears. She really loved him, because he had worked at it!

LOVE WILL BRING US TOGETHER:
  TO STRUGGLE TOGETHER
  TO WORK TOGETHER
  TO OVERCOME TOGETHER
  TO BE TOGETHER
  TO CRY TOGETHER
  TO LAUGH TOGETHER
  TO BUILD TOGETHER
  TO KISS AND HUG TOGETHER
  TO LOVE TOGETHER
   LOVE FINDS A WAY TO GET TOGETHER!

I heard someone tell this moving story. A young man in a midwestern city decided to leave home. He announced his intentions to his father and advised him that he would be leaving the next morning. "I have decided to leave," he said. "I am tired of your restraints and mother's pity." The night was long and restless for that father and mother. They loved their son, and were afraid of what might happen to him in a large city without their Christian counsel. All night they turned restlessly, and the stains of many tears were on the pillow.

The next morning, they heard their son tiptoeing down the stairs an hour before he usually arose. The father jumped out of bed and went to the head of the stairs and called out to the boy, who had already reached the front door. "Son, come in here a moment!" The boy turned back and walked slowly to his parents' room. His father put his arm gently, but firmly, around the boy's shoulder and said, "Son, your mother and I have not slept all night. We are sure that there must be something wrong in our lives, and before you go we want to ask you to forgive us." The boy looked into the weather-beaten face of his father, and saw the tears of love on his cheeks. "Father," the boy said, "the trouble is not with you and mother; the trouble is with me." Together they knelt by the bed and prayed. The boy got up with God's love flowing in his life. After that, home was the happiest place in the world for him.

LOVE WILL BRING US TOGETHER
AND
LOVE WILL KEEP US TOGETHER

DON'T BE AFRAID—LET GO—OPENLY EX-PRESS YOUR LOVE FOR ONE ANOTHER. I love to go home at the end of the day. It is the loviest, huggiest place on earth! Every morning when I leave and every evening when I return, there is hugging and kissing. This doesn't mean we always see eye to eye, or that things are always rosy or that there are never times of misunderstanding as imperfect people, learning to live together God's way. The sun never comes up or goes down without the Galloways touching and in some way expressing their love for one another. You see, the truth is I can afford no more failures in love. I have had all I want for my lifetime. I am determined, with God's help, to live out His marvelous love in our home. BECAUSE YOU HAVE FAILED IN THE PAST OR ARE FAILING NOW DOESN'T MEAN YOU CANNOT SUCCEED!

THIS VERY DAY...LOVE AGAIN!!
ONLY MORE!

BECAUSE
LOVE WILL BRING US TOGETHER!!

CHAPTER 9

Don't Let The Warts
Stop Your Love

Once upon a time there was a man who allowed the imperfections he saw in his pastor to stop his love cold. Over a period of time, as he withdrew his involvement and support from the church, he blamed his pastor for his spiritual cooling off. When he did manage to drag himself to the services, he would sit in the seat of the scornful and make himself believe that he was doing God a big favor by being there. The minute he left the church, with his family in the car, he would give himself a well deserved pat on the back, by telling his family members in a battery of negative remarks what was

wrong with the pastor. HOW BOGGED DOWN
AND DEFEATED GOOD PEOPLE CAN BE-
COME WHEN THEY ALLOW THEMSELVES TO
CENTER ON ANOTHER PERSON'S FAULTS.

For nine long years Aaron and Debra have
wanted to have a baby. Well, yesterday the long
anticipated day arrived and Debra gave birth to a 9
pound, 6 ounce baby boy. He is perfect in every
way, except that there is a birthmark over the top
of his right eye.

I would never have believed it if I had not seen it
and heard it myself. When Aaron and Debra saw
their first born, all they could see was the birthmark
over his right eye. Debra became so upset and
hysterical that she started shouting, "I don't want
him, I don't want him, he's got a horrible, hideous
wart. Take him back!" The last time I talked to
them they said that they wanted to give the baby
away for adoption because he had a wart. Can you
imagine that? Let me ask you—what do you think of
a couple who would reject a lovable, innocent little
baby just because he has a little bitty birthmark?
Terrible, isn't it?

To relieve your mind, let me tell you that the
story didn't really happen. I made it up to illustrate
a point. Aren't you glad that it only happened in my
imagination? But I really do see this same tragic
story repeated, only in a different way, again and
again in real life. HOW MANY TIMES HAVE WE
LET THE WARTS, THE IMPERFECTIONS WE
SEE IN OTHERS STOP OUR LOVE?

What foolish, trivial—warts—we allow to stop our

flow of love to our fellow workers, neighbors, church members, and family members. Things like:
Stubborn Pride
Human Faults
Prejudice
Difference of Opinion
And
Our Own Feelings of Inferiority
In the Bible we read this magnificent and magnanimous verse,

"LOVE OVERLOOKS A
MULTITUDE OF FAULTS."
TEN STEPS TO TAKE TO KEEP
OTHERS' FAULTS FROM STOPPING
YOUR FLOW OF LOVE.

1. REFUSE TO PICK AT ANOTHER PERSON'S WEAK SPOTS. In reading an article about turkeys, I learned from a turkey expert that when a turkey is wounded and has a spot of blood on it's feathers, the other turkeys will peck at that spot until they literally peck the wounded turkey to death. When I read that my first reaction was, "How cruel!" My second thought was, "How dumb turkeys must be to keep pecking at the wound of a fellow turkey." Man has the ability to be smart or dumb. You can be smart and refuse to pick at another's wound, or you can be as dumb as pecking turkeys.

Since picking is such a dumb thing for us to do, why then do we sometimes do it? To try to build up our own sinking ego we mistakenly think that by making the other guy look bad it makes us look good. The truth is that it makes us look worse than the guy we're trying to make look inferior. Picking always hurts the picker more than it hurts the picked. God's got a better way for you and me to live. It's called the way of love. "Love overlooks a multitude of faults." YES—SMARTER THAN A DUMB TURKEY—THAT'S YOU! GOD'S HAPPY LOVER!

2. RECOGNIZE THE FACT THAT NO ONE IS PERFECT. If you loved only perfect people, who would you love?

  Not me
  Not anyone at church
  Not your mate
  Not sinners
   and
  Certainly not yourself.

If you are a perfectionist God bless you but don't expect me to be perfect. The truth is that you are going to be a lot happier person when you learn to stop expecting other people to be perfect. Someone said, "The seed of discontent is in the expectation." One rule that I try to follow in my life is to always expect more of myself than I do of others. Whenever you get this turned around and expect more of others than we do of ourselves, we soon become an unhappy, miserable, fault-finder. It has always amazed me how little education, how little experience it takes to become a self-appointed critic. The one thing that we all have in common is that we make mistakes. Jesus said to those who were

123

accusing the adulterous woman, "Let him that is without sin cast the first stone." (John 8:7).

3. LEAVE THE JUDGING TO GOD! I've been having a little trouble recently with some traffic tickets. I'm actually a pretty good driver, when I'm thinking about it, but my weakness is that, too often, I drive with my mind on some great idea that God has given me. Though I'm trying to do better, please pray for me, because I need it! As I was sitting in the courtroom watching this one particular judge he gave the appearance of being the most unhappy man I've ever seen. As I watched him in action it seemed like he took the devil's delight in treating everyone like they were the scum of the earth. I thought to myself I pity the person who has to be judged by him.

Later in the day I thought, "I imagine judging can be a tough job. You would see some of the raunchiest things day after day." If being in the legal role of a judge can fill a man with such contempt for his fellow man, think what it does to us every time we assume the role of judge. Judging is not our role to fulfill. IT WAS A GREAT DAY FOR ME WHEN EARLY IN MY MINISTRY I LEARN-ED THE LESSON THAT AS A MINISTER I AM NOT YOUR JUDGE!

Jesus said, "DON'T CRITICIZE, and you won't be criticized. For others will treat you as you treat them. And why worry about a speck in the eye of a brother, when you have a board in your own? Should you say, 'Friend, let me help you get that speck out of your eye,' when you can't even see because of the board in your own? Hypocrite! First,

124

get rid of the board. Then you can see to help your brother." (Matt. 7:1-5, TLB).

4. CONFESS YOUR OWN FAULTS. The harsh spirit of fault-finding and being judgmental of another evaporates the instant I become aware of my own faults and have the courage to confess them openly in the family of believers. Confession is good for what ails you. It is the step you must take if God is to heal you of being a fault-finder. The scripture is very clear as to what we are to do when it urges us in James, "Confess your faults one to another, and pray for one another, that you might be healed." (James 5:16). For healing to take place in our inner spirits, two things must happen: We must confess our own faults and we must respond to the other guy's faults by praying for him. As we do this, God promises that we will be healed and our attitudes will be wholesome and our relationships will be whole.

CONFESS NO ONE'S FAULTS BUT YOUR OWN. But, confess your own faults that you might be healed. Healed of what?

Healed of fault-finding
Healed of knit-picking.
Healed of judging
Healed of jumping to wrong conclusions.
Healed of backbiting.
Healed of malicious gossip.
Healed of picking at other's faults.

Confess your faults—that you might be healed of what ails you!

5. ACCEPT THE OTHER PERSON'S RIGHT TO BE DIFFERENT. How many times do we shut

someone out of our circle simply because they are a little different than we are.   STRETCH YOUR LOVE BY RECOGNIZING THAT THERE ARE:

Day people and night people.
Tidy people and not-so-tidy people
Men and Women.
Pork eaters and beef eaters.
Those who like sports and those who don't.

DON'T WITHHOLD YOUR LOVE FROM EVERYONE WHO IS A LITTLE DIFFERENT THAN YOU ARE BECAUSE IF YOU DO THERE WILL BE NO ONE FOR YOU TO LOVE. Some people are so exclusive, so narrow-minded that their ears touch each other. Love never excludes— it always reaches out and includes. Someone has said it so well in this little poem:

"He drew a circle that shut me out,
Heretic, rebel, a thing to flout,
But love and I had the wit to win;
We drew a circle that took him in!"

YES, LOVE STRETCHES AND FREES US
TO LOVE PERSONS
WHO ARE DIFFERENT THAN WE ARE!

6. DON'T FALL INTO THE TRIVIALITY TRAP. 99% of the things that upset people today are really petty. You can save yourself a lot of heartburn by asking yourself this question: "IS IT REALLY THAT IMPORTANT?" Is the fact that he didn't put the cap on the toothpaste really worth getting all steamed up about? WHAT TRIVIAL THINGS WE ALLOW TO STOP OUR LOVE!

A remarkable mother shared, with my wife and me, what happened between her teenage boy and herself. The teenage son, who we will call Jerry, was a real neat kid and wanted to be in the forefront of changing styles. So he decided he wanted to wear his hair long. This was back a couple of years ago when most conservative church people associated long hair with the hippie life-style. For her son to have long hair was a social embarrassment, she felt, whenever they were with their church friends. Besides, the sight of long hair on her son personally irritated her.

Unable to keep quiet about the matter, the mother straight forwardly told her son that she disapproved of his hairstyle. But added that she had an open mind about it and that if he would agree to it they would both make it a matter of prayer in their lives. (She thought that surely God would change her son's mind.)

As the mother persisted in calling upon God to give her an answer in this matter that seemed so gigantic to her the answer came in a very unexpected way. God chose to give her the answer as she viewed a live drama taking place, before her very eyes, on a downtown street. She witnessed another teenage boy, about her son's age, and his mother having a fight in front of everyone. The teenage boy shouted ugly words at his mother and showed his utter contempt and disrespect for her in front of a gathered crowd of onlookers. At that very moment the Christian mother bowed her head and thanked God for her wonderful boy; for his respect, good manners, and most of all the love that he gave to his mother. God had given her the answer. It wasn't the length of her son's hair that mattered after all. What counted most was the love and the right relationship that they enjoyed as mother and son.

Later that evening, when the son came home from ball practice, the mother asked him if he had received any answer to his prayer about what God thought concerning the length of his hair. He replied that he felt very uncomfortable with the length of his hair. Enthusiastically, the mother shared the answer that God had given to her. It is absolutely dumbfounding what prayers are answered when we ourselves are willing to let God change us!

As this appealing Christian mother finished sharing the lesson that God had taught her she pointed to her son, who was about twenty feet away from where she was seated, and proundly exclaimed, "That's my boy!" My wife, Margi, commented, "What a handsome, clean-cut young man in that modish hairdo." We all enjoyed a good laugh.

LOVE CENTERS ON
WHAT REALLY COUNTS
AND REFUSES TO BE BLOCKED OUT
BY OPINIONS AND PREJUDICES.

7. BE PATIENT AND KIND. AREN'T YOU GLAD THAT GOD IS PATIENT WITH US? In (I Corinthians 13:4, we read, "Love is patient and kind." Not only are we to be patient but kind. When

we are truly patient the remarks come out of kindness and not cutting. In Romans we are given this word of advice, "We then that are strong ought to bear the infirmities of the weak and not to please ourselves." (Romans 15:1).

8. STOP TRYING TO CHANGE THE OTHER PERSON. When you are always trying to change the other person you are saying, to that person, "to me you are unacceptable." One of our greatest needs is to feel accepted. If you really love a person you want to help him and the way you help him is not by trying to change him but by accepting that person as someone of worth and value. Treat the other person like a somebody and you will be absolutely amazed at what wonderful changes will take place.

9. PRACTICE FORGIVENESS. HOW HAVE YOU HANDLED THE FLAWS YOU SEE IN ANOTHER PERSON'S LIFE? A man or woman never stands taller than when he practices "Be kind to each other, tenderhearted, forgiving one another, just as God has forgiven you because you belong to Christ." (Ephesians 4:32, TLB). How are we to practice forgiveness? Just as God has forgiven us.

TO ERR IS HUMAN
TO FORGIVE IS DIVINE.

The story is told about John D. Rockefeller, the tycoon, who built the great Standard Oil empire. It seems that Rockefeller was a man who demanded high performance from his companies' executives.

One day one of the executives made a $2 million mistake. The news of this man's enormous error soon spread through the executives. During this entire day these men made themselves scarce and were afraid to even go near John D. Rockefeller's office for fear of his reaction towards this mistake. But one brave executive decided he would go ahead and keep his appointment and go in to see John Rockefeller. As he walked in the door the oil monarch was writing on a piece of paper but soon looked up and abruptly said, "I guess you have heard about the $2 million mistake our friend made." "Yes," he said, expecting Rockefeller to explode at any moment. Then Rockefeller said, "I've been listing all of the good qualities of our friend, here on a sheet of paper, and I've discovered that in the past he has made us many times more than the amount he lost for us today by his one mistake. His good points so far outweigh this one human error that I think we ought to forgive him, don't you?" Yes, forgiveness is what it takes to really love and overlook a multitude of faults!

10. REMEMBER LOVE IS MAGNANIMOUS. It looks at people in the best light. It looks for the good and overlooks the bad. Love sees the grand possibilities in the other person, and then proceeds to bring the best out of that person. LOVE IS NOT BIGHEADED—BUT IT IS BIGHEARTED!

LOVE IS AN EVER PRESENT—BEAUTIFUL— POSSIBILITY! God has given you love to give to others. So, don't block it; don't stop it! WHATEVER YOU DO—DON'T LET THE WARTS STOP YOUR LOVE. If your love is stopped you have no one to put the finger of blame on except yourself. NO ONE CAN STOP YOUR LOVE FROM FLOWING—BUT YOU!

"Do you like dollies?" the little girl asked her house guest. "Yes, very much," the man responded. "Then I'll show you mine," was the reply. Thereupon she presented one by one a whole family of dolls. "And now tell me," the visitor asked, "Which is your favorite doll?" The child hesitated for a moment and then she said, "You're quite sure you like dollies, and will you please promise not to smile if I show you my favorite?" The man solemnly promised and the girl hurried from the room. In a moment she returned with a tattered and dilapidated old doll. It's hair had come off; it's nose was broken; it's cheeks were scratched; an arm and a leg were missing. "Well, well," said the visitor, "and why do you like this one best?" "I love her most," said the little girl, "Because if I didn't love her, no one else would." (R. E. Thomas)

YOU, MY FRIEND, ARE CHOSEN BY GOD
TO LOVE.
THERE ARE PEOPLE WHO
DESPERATELY NEED YOUR LOVE!
SO, DON'T LET THE WARTS
STOP YOUR LOVE.
LET—LOVE FLOW!!

CHAPTER 10

Can Love Be Repaired?

During the past two months we have been experiencing a parade of repairmen coming to our home.

First—the dryer went capooie so, we called a dryer repairman and he came out and fixed it for a stinging amount of money.

Next—our dishwasher broke down so, we called a dishwasher repairman and he came out and fixed it for what I thought was an exorbitant fee.

In a few days—Our furnace was leaking gas so, we called the furnace repairman and he came out and although he didn't do much he gave us a gigantic bill.

Then—our stereo stopped, and since it was getting close to Christmas, we had to get it fixed—You guessed it! The repairman ripped us off for another thirty bucks!

Well—This week our garage door opener went on the blink—so, guess what happened? We had a garage door repairman come out. How much do you think he charged? Ah! We lucked out—he was a friend and he did it for free!

Hopefully everything in our home has been repaired now and should be in great working order for awhile. As I write this, I have my fingers crossed. Since our parade of repairmen, I have been thinking about all the breakdowns in love between persons. What would a person be willing to pay to have a broken relationship repaired? In perspective, the breakdown of a machine is a little, bitty thing—compared to the breakdown of love in a relationship. Question: CAN LOVE BE REPAIRED?

CAN TWO PEOPLE FALL IN LOVE AGAIN?

Once the Osbornes were so in love that they were inseparable. But now two kids and many disappointments later they are two strangers living in the same house. It is not often that they even speak to each other but when they do their voices are filled with animosity.

The lonely man is becoming a "work-aholic"—all

because he is trying to avoid spending uncomfortable evenings at home. About the only time he goes home anymore is when he thinks his wife will already be in bed asleep.

At home, his distraught wife takes out her frustrations on the dog and their two kids. She is now certain that she is a martyr. Her bucket of self-pity and truckload of bitterness keep her supplied with the daily hostility that drives her husband further and further away from her.

The Osbornes' two children are torn up on the inside by the tug-of-war that is going on between their parents. The junior-high boy, in recent months, has become rebellious and is already a potential drop-out, while the seven-year-old girl continues to suck her thumb and wet the bed out of her inner feelings of insecurity which she gets from the unstable atmosphere at home. YOU HAD BETTER BELIEVE IT—WHEN LOVE IS LACKING IN A MARRIAGE—IT NOT ONLY HURTS THE MAN AND THE WOMAN, BUT IT DAMAGES THE CHILDREN EMOTIONALLY!

There are countless situations like the one I have described. "Is there any hope for my marriage?" the woman asked me after telling me that she thought she was in love with another man. "Yes," I said, "THERE IS HOPE!! I have seen many husbands and wives fall in love all over again." She said, "What if I didn't even love him when I married him?" I said, "Even if you have never loved him, you can fall in love with your husband for the first time."

JESUS IS OUR HOPE. Thanks be unto God we

134

are not hopeless or without hope. This is what the Bible is all about! How God in love sent Jesus to repair our broken hearts and broken relationships. Jesus has come to break down all the walls of contempt that separate us from God, and from each other. In your life and in your marriage let Jesus Christ replace:

Guilt with forgiveness
Despair with hope
Conflict with peace
Loneliness with togetherness
Jesus will give you love—love—sweet love!!

YES, WITH JESUS
AS YOUR REPAIRMAN
YOU CAN LOVE EACH OTHER
AGAIN—AND AGAIN!

SIX STEPS TO TAKE TO FIX
A BROKEN RELATIONSHIP

1. BE COMMITTED TO JESUS CHRIST AND HIS LIFE-STYLE. There are two kinds of people in this world. Troublemakers and peacemakers. You can be either one you choose. The choice is yours. However, if you are going to be a true disciple of Jesus there is only one right choice for you to make. Jesus said, "Blessed are the peacemakers for they shall be called the children of God." (Matthew 5:9).

2. ADMIT YOUR OWN WRONG. No matter what the other person said about you, no matter

what names they called you, no matter how badly they mistreated you, no matter how deeply they have wounded your pride, the other person's wrong attitudes or actions are no excuse for your wrong attitudes and actions.

Charles Spurgeon used to tell this story: "A certain duke once boarded a galley ship. As he passed the crew of slaves, he asked several of them what their offenses were. Almost every man claimed he was innocent. They laid the blame on someone else or accused the judge of yielding to bribery. One young fellow, however, spoke out, 'Sir, I deserve to be here. I stole the money. No one is at fault but myself. I'm guilty!' Upon hearing this, the duke seized him by the shoulder and shouted, 'You scoundrel, you! What are you doing here with all these dishonest men? Get out of their company at once!' He was then set at liberty while the rest were left to tug at the oars."

3. FORGIVE AND FORGET. Have you ever wondered why some people can never maintain a relationship. Could it be because they allow themselves to be too easily hurt and once hurt they cling to their hurts like it was their very best friend? Stubbornly, they refuse to forgive the other person. As a minister I have seen the saddest most tragic things happen to persons who refuse to forgive.

THERE ARE NO ENDURING RELATION-SHIPS WITHOUT A TRAINLOAD OF FORGIVE-NESS. Mark it down, if you know someone long enough, and if you are a sensitive person at all, sometime, either intentionally or unintentionally

136

that person is going to say something or do something that hurts your feelings. That's the fact of life. That's the way it is. Many times it is not because the person means to hurt you, in fact, most of the hurts that people suffer are not intentionally inflicted.

FORGIVENESS IS THE FOUNDATION FOR ALL CONTINUING RELATIONSHIPS. FORGIVENESS IS THE HIGHEST EXPRESSION OF LOVE!

FORGIVE OTHERS. DO IT NOT ONLY FOR THEIR SAKES BUT FOR YOUR OWN. If you don't you'll experience nauseating resentment destroying you from within. It was of interest to me to discover that in some societies and cultures physical scars are looked upon as symbols of bravery. But around the world emotional scars always hurt. Without forgiveness we go on hurting, and hurting.

But it's not easy to forgive—to forgive a person who has hurt you. A good part of the time people are not even aware they have hurt us. Is it right to hurt deeply on the inside and not give any indication to the person who has hurt us, not give them a chance to know our true feelings? WHAT ARE ALTERNATIVES TO PRACTICING FORGIVENESS?

ONE IS TO CARRY A GRUDGE. You can

nourish it; you can think about the wrong done to you. You can become bitter. If you choose to, you can always find a reason to carry a grudge. The reason doesn't have to be large. But no matter how large or small, it will wreck your spirits and add fuel to the fire of a broken relationship.

ANOTHER ALTERNATIVE IS REVENGE. You can strike back at the person who has hurt you. You can try to even things up. You may try to make them pay. But the moment we try to even things up, we compound our problems by adding explosive fuel to the fire.

STILL ANOTHER ALTERNATIVE IS JUST TO BURY IT. Act as if it didn't happen when you know it did happen. There is very little healing that can take place by doing this. Actually the only solution to deep pain is to forgive. Forgiveness is the only thing that can bring healing and release. When we find it hard to forgive it is because we enjoy feeling condemned. We get a morbid satisfaction from it. One thing is for certain! It doesn't do us any good!

Can you imagine what a task it would be to carry a heavy crate of oranges around on your back all day long? It would be impossible to relax. One can never relax while carrying feelings of resentment or grudges or just an unwillingness to forgive. It is only when we forgive that we can stop being uptight and enjoy living. Forgiveness is divine! It comes from God. It is His gift to us. It is the willingness to say, "Let's begin again. I'll give you another chance. I'll love you in spite of . . . " It always brings the best out of both the giver and the receiver. It is the way to have continuing, growing relationships!

138

THE ONE WHO POSSESSES
GOD'S KIND OF LOVE—FORGIVES!

It is so easy to love people who are good, who do the right thing, and say the right thing. But what about when they don't act right? What about when they hurt you? I want to tell you that God has healing for all of your hurts. I think of the young woman who was filled with hate for her husband who was running around with another woman. You know there is more than one way to kill love in a marriage. It wasn't until the day she stopped blaming and condemning him for his wrongs, and faced her own failures, that she received God's forgiveness and then was able to forgive her husband. As she received God's love and forgiveness and in turn began to express that love and forgiveness towards her husband, she won him back. FORGIVENESS WINS A RECONCILIATION!

GOD'S HEALING MEDICINE
IS YOURS
FOR THE USING!

FORGIVENESS MEANS PUTTING IT BEHIND YOU. A couple came into their pastor's office to discuss some marriage problems they were having and as they talked the woman kept bringing up things that had happened. The man said, "Look, Alice, I thought you promised to forget all that; you'd forgiven me." "Yes, but I want you to remember that I've forgotten."

If we really forgive out of a loving heart, then we

are not going to want to bring up those same old hurts again. To do so is to only add pain and to peck away at what is a new beginning. Now this doesn't mean that it is not going to come to mind. You can't just say, "I forget it" and expect it to never come up again. Because of associations and things that happen it will all come back again. This is where discipline of the mind comes in. We need to just reconfirm the fact, "I have forgiven. God's helped me to forgive. I want to forgive and I'm just not going to throw it up to the person anymore. I'm going to put it behind me and go from here." Time does heal a heart that has been open and honest and forgiving.

4. PRAY FOR THE OTHER PERSON. Do you know that prayer actually does change the way the other person looks at you? Prayer creates the atmosphere that is needed to bring people back together again. PRAYER WORKS MIRACLES BETWEEN PEOPLE!

5. ASK THE OTHER PERSON TO FORGIVE YOU. We have heard from the Gospel that sinners need to ask for forgiveness and change their style of life. If we are not careful we come to the conclusion that only "sinners"need to ask for forgiveness. But it is true that every person who lives, no matter how good or bad he may be, is involved in the process of both giving and receiving forgiveness.

I'd just as well confess that in my own life I stand in need of forgiveness. I find that I often hurt people whom I do not intend or set out to hurt. It's a part of the human situation. But I need to confess it and let God bring healing.

EACH OF US IS CONSTANTLY IN NEED OF FORGIVENESS!

BE THE FIRST TO ASK FOR FORGIVENESS. When you do, don't make the mistake of talking about anyone's wrong doing but your own. Simply state what your wrong attitude or action has been and ask the other person to forgive you in a way that they must respond. Whether they forgive you or not is up to them. You have done what is the right thing for you to do.

6. OVERCOME EVIL BY DOING GOOD. A couple of years ago there was an individual with whom my wife, Margi, felt a strained relationship. Margi tried hard to recall any incident which may have occurred and caused hurt to the other person but she could not think of any. Yet, the vibrations came through that "you are my enemy—not my friend." Do you know what Margi did? She did some of the nicest things you could do for another person. She showered this person with friendship and love. As a result—she eliminated an enemy by making this individual a friend! YOU—TOO—CAN WIN ALL YOUR PRIVATE WARS—WITH LOVE!!

WHAT DO YOU DO WHEN YOU HAVE DONE YOUR BEST TO FIX THE RELATIONSHIP AND THE OTHER PERSON REJECTS YOU—AND YOUR LOVE? ACCEPT WHAT YOU CANNOT CHANGE.

From my own experience and from others I have learned that there are some broken relationships that—try as you will—cannot be repaired, simply because the relationship involves not only you, but another person. Each person has a will of his own. For a relationship that has been broken to be repaired, it takes two people who are willing to work at it—to forgive and to respond. MOST IMPORTANT—I AM RESPONSIBLE ONLY FOR MY OWN ATTITUDES AND ACTIONS. NOT THE OTHER PERSON'S. There have been many times in my relationships when I have had to pray this PRAYER OF SERENITY:

GOD, GRANT ME THE SERENITY
TO ACCEPT THE THINGS I CANNOT CHANGE;
THE COURAGE TO CHANGE
THE THINGS I CAN;
AND THE WISDOM TO KNOW
THE DIFFERENCE.

In one of our Sunday evening fellowship and praise services, during the time in which Christians minister to each other, Tom Zimmerman, one of our young men of the church who is just really a fantastic guy, stood and shared this little anecdote:

It seems that their little five-year-old started feeling his Cheerios and had said some rather sassy things back to his mother. His father, Tom, became concerned that this unacceptable behavior be corrected without delay. So, he decided to have a fatherly talk with the boy. The boy, in a way quite characteristic of us all, wanted to blame his misbehavior on his sister, his mother, and his father. Tom explained to him that it wasn't his father's fault, it wasn't his mother's fault, and it wasn't his sister's fault but that he alone was responsible for his misbehavior. Tom told him that each of us decides for himself how he will act, what he will say, and what he won't say.

Not to be outdone, the little guy immediately replied, "It must have been the devil that made me do it." Thereupon, the father firmly pronounced the sentence, "The devil or not the devil, you are never to talk this way again to your parents. As your father I will not tolerate disrespectful talk to the woman I love."

The little guy then took a sheet of paper and wrote a letter to the devil. It said, "Dear Devil," and then across the paper he wrote as large as he could write, "N-O, NO!! SAY NO TO THE DEVIL."

LET GOD HEAL YOUR BROKEN HEART. God specializes in making the wounded whole. In the Old Testament it speaks of a balm in Gilead that was applied to wounds that had a miraculous power to heal. To all your wounds let the Great Physician, Jesus, apply the balm of Gilead. Your job is to keep resentment and ill feeling out of the wounds. Remember it takes time for a wound to heal but God is going to make you whole again and when it happens you are going to be stronger and better off than ever!

NEVER GIVE UP HOPE. The Bible says, "Hope thou in God." Hope that this difficulty will soon pass. Hope that the storm will soon be over. Hope that the pain will soon be healed. Hope that you soon will be on the other side of the mountain. NEVER GIVE UP HOPE—BECAUSE THE BEST IS YET TO COME!

LOVE AGAIN, ONLY MORE! Because you have lost in love or suffered the hurt of a broken relationship don't bury your love. Don't withdraw from other people. Possibly you need to stay away from a person if that person is vindictive and openly trying to hurt you. But thank the Lord that not every person is filled with such hate and contempt. So, don't withdraw from everyone just because one person is hurting you. GOD'S WAY TO OVERCOME IS TO LOVE AGAIN—ONLY MORE!

GO AHEAD!
BREAK THROUGH THE BARRIER
AND
THRILL TO A RENEWAL OF LOVE

One of our new converts came into my office and was greatly disturbed over a question her grade school daughter had asked her. "Mother, do you love me?" The mother told me that since Jesus had come into her life she felt a whole new kind of love inside for her family members, but that she had never in her life been able to say to someone, "I love you." She told me that inside she loved her husband. He was a good man but that outwardly she treated him coldly and was totally unresponsive to him as a husband. She wanted to know how to break through the barriers that she had lived with

144

all of her life. "How do I let my new true feelings of love be expressed to my family members?" I talked to her about her need to ask her husband particularly and also her other family members to forgive her for her failure to express love. We prayed together and asked Jesus Christ, the love repairman, to fix her relationship with her husband and children. Here is the letter that I received from her the following Sunday:

"Dear Dale and Margi:

I want to express my thanks to both of you for giving so freely of your love. At first, I could not believe that two people could love so much and care about others as you do but I know in my heart your love and friendship are true. I took your advice, Pastor, and told my husband I was sorry and that I loved him. I didn't do it that same day but instead, I read from the Bible, I Corinthians 13. The next day I let my true feelings come forth. What a beautiful experience it has become. It seems like I can't stop telling my husband and children how much I love them. One of the hardest things for me to do was to admit I was wrong. Once I did, it seemed like everything around me changed. To express my feeling of thanks to Jesus, I wrote these few words and would like to share them with you:

'Jesus planted the seed of love into our hearts.
It's roots are growing strong and deep.
It's blossoms have filled the air with a peace
    like none I have ever known.
Thank you, Jesus, for turning our house into
    a home!' "

DON'T LET ANYONE OR ANYTHING KEEP
YOU FROM GIVING YOUR LOVE TO LOVED
ONES.

SAY IT!
EXPRESS IT!
LET IT OUT!
GIVE IT OUT!

DO WHAT GOD HAS DONE—GIVE THEM
ALL YOUR LOVE!

CHAPTER 11

Speaking The Truth In Love

I don't think that my life will ever be the same again because of what God has been teaching me about His kind of love. The step of love that I am now going to share with you is a most difficult one to master but has boundless possibilities for your spiritual growth and development. You must know by now that the most magnificent mountain peaks of love are never completely conquered. But with the huge strides and advancements that many of you have been making in your impressive journey of love, I believe that you are now ready to commence climbing to the top of one of the super summits of love.

THE DEEPEST, MOST SATISFYING RELA-
TIONSHIPS BETWEEN PERSONS ARE BUILT
WITH THE UNBEATABLE COMBINATION OF
TRUTH AND LOVE. Anyone who builds their
relationships on anything less than openness and
honesty is not building for permanency. It's like the
man about whom Jesus spoke who built his house on
quicksand. When stresses and pressures come—as
they always do—the relationship crumbles. Unfortunately, many relationships are predestined to
crumble because they have been built on the
quicksand of deception and deceit.

GOD HAS A MUCH MORE ENDURING WAY
FOR US TO RELATE. IT IS THE OPEN
METHOD OF TRUTH AND LOVE. In Ephesians
4:15, we are challenged, "Let us speak the truth in
love; so shall we fully grow up in Christ." (N.E.B.)
When this verse is properly applied in one's life and
relationships the results are well worth the extra
effort.

HOW WOULD YOU LIKE TO HAVE:
GOOD MENTAL HEALTH?
CONTINUING GROWTH AND DEVELOP-
MENT AS A PERSON?
GROWING FULFILLING RELATIONSHIPS
WITH OTHERS?
HELP OTHER PEOPLE BLOOM WHERE
THEY ARE PLANTED?

Even though the results of learning to speak the
truth in love in relationships is stupendous, let me

be the first to admit that I am still in the process of learning how to speak the truth in love. Speaking the truth in love has never been and still is not easy for me to do. Partly because I want everyone to love me and partly because I am very sensitive about not wanting to hurt another person's feelings. Because of this there are many times when I should speak up but I find myself holding back the truth. The other side of the coin is that it is not the easiest thing in the world for me to receive the truth—the whole truth and nothing but the bare truth—about myself, even when it is spoken in love. But because I have a great desire to climb to the heights of love I am asking Jesus to give me the courage to take steps that will teach me how to effectively "Truth it—in love" in all my relationships.

EVERY CHRISTIAN WAS BORN TO GROW UP IN CHRIST. Learning to speak and to receive the truth in love is necessary for our growth and development as Christians. How can I move beyond where I am at this moment unless truth shows me the way to advance? The New Testament concept of the church is that we are all members of the same family. In Christ we belong to one another and make tremendous spiritual advances as we help one another. Any time one of the family grows more into the likeness of Jesus, we all grow. It is only in such a circle of concern and love for one another that persons can dare to open themselves up to one another to speak and to hear the shaping-up truth. The one principle that we are to always follow in our relationships with one another can be summed up in one word: "edification." As members of the fellowship of believers we are to build one another up in God's kind of love.

> *HONESTY AND OPENNESS IS*
> *HIS MORE MATURE WAY*
> *FOR US TO RELATE.*

Do you like to be lied to? No.
Do you like to be deceived? No.
Do you like to be given only half the truth? No.
Do you appreciate being the victim of any kind of
   deception? No.

> *JESUS SAID,*
> *"TREAT OTHERS LIKE YOU*
> *WANT TO BE TREATED."*
> *TO TELL THE TRUTH IS THE*
> *GREATEST KINDNESS YOU CAN DO.*

Lying and deception are not new with modern politicians. Dishonesty is ancient history. Jeremiah, the prophet, said thousands of years ago, "The heart is deceitful above all things, and desperately wicked; who can know it?" (Jeremiah 17:9). The pages of any history book are filled with man's lies and deception.

DISHONESTY IS STILL A HARD ROAD TO TRAVEL. All the results of dishonesty are undesirable. One lie leads to many others. Lying destroys self-respect. Sooner or later a lie will always have a way of coming back to haunt and trouble the liar. Lying and deception destroy trust

150

in the relationship in a way that often cannot be repaired for many years. The Bible said, "a false witness shall not be unpunished: and he that speaketh lies shall not escape." (Proverbs 19:5). When we think about it we realize that there is not one lasting advantage to telling a lie. I wonder why, then, in the name of reason, people do so much of it? One thing that I like about telling the truth is that I don't have to worry about remembering who I talked to last!

The truth is that our society is shot through with dishonesty. For many, lying has become a way of life. This is not God's good way for us to live. God's way is so much better than Satan's. Satan is a deceiver and a liar and has been using deception to mess people up for thousands and thousands of years. As followers of Jesus we have become new and different people and since we are now holy and good we are to clothe ourselves with a new nature and, "Stop lying to each other; tell the truth, for we are parts of each other and when we lie to each other we are hurting ourselves." (Ephesians 4:25, TLB).

QUESTION: HOW CAN ONE BECOME AN OPEN HONEST PERSON IN THE MIDST OF SO MUCH SHAME AND DISHONESTY? I believe it takes an inner transformation of one's very nature. The Bible calls this conversion. The starting point for becoming an honest and open person is when we fall on our knees before God and confess our sins and ask Jesus to forgive us. Never is a man more honest than when he becomes a confessing sinner. WHAT LIFE CHANGING MIRACLES JESUS

WORKS! CHANGING DISHONEST, HIDING SINNERS INTO HONEST, OPEN SAINTS!

It is as we become wide open and honest with God that there comes the courage to build open Christian relationships with other persons. A Christian relationship is one that is built upon speaking the truth in love. It is this kind of relationship that will endure in increasing mutual benefits with the years.

OPENNESS TO GOD—OPENS US
UP TO OTHERS!

WHEN SHOULD YOU
SPEAK THE TRUTH IN LOVE?

1. WHEN A FRIEND ASKS FOR YOUR HELP. Often we human beings cannot see the forest for the trees. In my first pastorate a young couple was having a great deal of difficulty with their little toddler. It was evident to everyone that he was controlling his parents by throwing tantrums. In desperation one day the mother said to me, "Pastor, I just don't know what to do when Johnny throws himself on the floor and kicks and screams. Could you tell me what to do?" I looked her right in the eye and said, "Are you sure you want me to tell you?" She pleaded with me, "Please, do!" I said, "The next time he tries that bit of foolishness, pick him up, put him over your knee, and spank the daylights out of him. Spank him until you break his defiant will. Then hold him close and tenderly love him." Well, she took my advice and I think after

that Johnny had about two more tantrums and that was the end of them!

A RELATIONSHIP
THAT CANNOT WITHSTAND
"TRUTH SPOKEN IN LOVE"
WILL NOT SURVIVE ANYWAY.

2. YOU SHOULD SPEAK THE TRUTH WHEN YOU HAVE A CLOSE RELATIONSHIP WITH ANOTHER PERSON AND YOU SEE THAT WHAT YOU ARE GOING TO SAY TO HELP HIM HAS A GOOD CHANCE OF BEING RECEIVED. Two girls from opposite parts of America were thrown together as roommates at a small midwestern college. It wasn't long until they struck up a close friendship. One girl, Katie, was afflicted with a very low self-image. The fact that she had been brought up in a very negative church had not helped her with these negative feelings about herself but only served to intensify her feeling of being ugly and unacceptable. Her new friend, Eloise, was just the opposite. She was full of self-confidence, outgoing, and enjoyed good feelings about herself. As she was being brought up her parents and church nurtured her on good feelings about herself as a person of worth and value who God loved!

As the two girls lived together week after week and month after month, Katie's continual negative remarks about herself began to irritate Eloise. It was difficult for her to understand why her roommate, who had been endowed with so much natural physical beauty, would have to make a negative remark about her appearance every time she went near a mirror. One day as Eloise was reading in the Old Testament, she read the words in Proverbs, "Wounds from a friend are better than kisses from an enemy." (Proverbs 27:6, TLB) As she meditated and talked to her Heavenly Father on the truth of this verse she made a decision that for the good of her friend, for the good of her own mental health, and for the good of their friendship she would speak the truth in love to Katie.

Eloise, using good common sense, watched for just the right moment when Katie and she were in their room together alone to speak the truth in love. Using tact she said, "Katie do you know that many girls in this dormitory are envious of the physical beauty that God has given you? But beyond your physical beauty I found that you have many marvelous characteristics of personality and I have come to really love you as a sister. But...there is one thing that I can't understand. I am puzzled as to why you keep running down a beautiful person that God has created. It just makes me feel awful to hear you keep calling yourself the 'ugly duck'."

First Katie took offense to what her roommate was saying but after shedding a few tears she was able to thank Eloise and to admit that she had a very low self-image and needed help. She promised to stop running herself down all of the time and then asked her friend to remind her, whenever she slipped, of her commitment to do better. Years have passed since that day and, although the girls live miles apart, they are still the best of friends.

SOME OF OUR GREATEST
GROWTH AND DEVELOPMENT
AS GOD'S CHILDREN
FOLLOWS A LITTLE PLAIN
PAINING TRUTH
SPOKEN IN LOVE BY A FRIEND.

3.   YOU SHOULD SPEAK THE TRUTH IN
LOVE WHEN THE OTHER PERSON IS HURT-
ING YOU. I ask you—is it fair to build resentment
against another person for something they are
doing or not doing when they are unaware of what is
happening?   In every relationship there comes a
time when the air needs to be cleared. One thing I
appreciate about my wife, Margi, is that if I do
something that she doesn't like it is not long until
she tells me. I find her an easy person with whom to
live because I don't have to continually guess what it
is that I might be doing that is bothering her. You
see, when I know what it is I can respond by telling
my side of it or accepting the fact that I need to
make a change. It is through open exchange that
understanding and improvement can result.

How many times something a person does
irritates us or bothers us and we choose to keep
silent telling ourselves that we do not want to make
waves. What we are really doing is storing a stick
of dynamite inside. The next day something else is
done that is upsetting and nothing is said. So, that
puts dynamite stick number two inside. A couple of
hours later we put dynamite stick number three in
storage and a few days later dynamite stick number

four. Now everybody's tolerance level is different but each of us has a limit as to how much dynamite we can store before the big blowup. My tolerance level is about ten sticks of dynamite and then a little dinky thing happens and the fuse is lit and BOOM, BOOM, BOOM! I have an emotional explosion. When the dust settles I am ashamed of my actions and I find it hard to believe that I became so angry and upset over such a trivial thing. It all started back there, a week ago, when I didn't say anything because I didn't want to make waves.

TO AVOID EMOTIONAL BLOWUPS
GO AHEAD AND
MAKE SOME LITTLE WAVES.
SPEAK THE TRUTH IN LOVE
WHEN THE
DAILY IRRITATIONS OCCUR.

Speaking the truth in love is not attacking the other person. To the contrary. It is simply reporting your own feelings. For example, "This is the way I feel." "This is my viewpoint." "I don't know who is wrong and who is right here but this is the way it affects me." WHATEVER YOU DO—DO NOT BLAME OR ATTACK THE OTHER PERSON. SIMPLY REPORT ON YOUR OWN FEELINGS.

CARE ENOUGH ABOUT YOUR OWN
EMOTIONAL HEALTH
TO SPEAK
YOUR TRUE FEELINGS IN LOVE.

4. YOU SHOULD SPEAK THE TRUTH IN LOVE WHEN A FRIEND WHO VALUES YOUR OPINION IS HURTING SOMEONE ELSE ABOUT WHOM YOU CARE. Oftentimes, in the family relationship, one mate will see something that the other mate is doing that is hurting one of their children. In a case such as this speaking the truth in love to the mate can be a great help to everyone concerned. What advantage there is if we can learn from one another! When a parent observes that one of the children has a bad attitude and is upsetting the entire household, he should speak the truth in love to the child in private. The truth is that as we live in love we can help and be helped by one another.

NEVER CONFRONT A PERSON
IN PUBLIC
DO YOUR CONFRONTATION
IN PRIVATE.

5. YOU SHOULD SPEAK THE TRUTH IN LOVE WHEN YOU SEE A MEMBER OF YOUR CHURCH HURTING THE BODY OF CHRIST. In the Bible we learn that the unity of a church is most important. We are not free to do our own thing if it means hurting the positive spirit of love in the fellowship. As you know bad attitudes are contagious. Negative remarks can stop the flow of positive love. As followers of Jesus, it becomes each of our responsibility to do everything in our power to maintain the spirit of Christ in the church which

157

is love. It is not the site, or the size that makes a local church great, but the spirit—positive loving spirit! Maintaining the spirit means sometimes speaking the truth in love to one another when we get out of line in our attitudes or remarks.

6. WHEN SHOULD YOU SPEAK THE TRUTH IN LOVE? NEVER SHOULD YOU SPEAK UNTIL THERE IS LOVE IN YOUR HEART! The truth without love is like a sledgehammer coming down on top of a person. It can do nothing but damage. But truth with love is like a beacon light guiding us to spiritual growth and continuing growing relationships. WHEN YOU ARE GOING TO SPEAK THE TRUTH MAKE SURE YOU DO IT IN LOVE BY FOLLOWING THESE FIVE GUIDELINES:

1. MAKE IT A POINT TO PRAY FOR THE OTHER PERSON, and about what it is that you feel you must speak to them before you ever open your mouth.

2. CHECK YOUR MOTIVES to be sure that they are constructive and not destructive. Only speak when your desire is to build the person up and not to hurt them or tear them down. Ask yourself, "Do I want to help this other person or hurt them?" Be brutally honest before God with yourself.

3. REMEMBER YOU DON'T HAVE GOD'S KIND OF LOVE IN YOUR HEART UNTIL YOU CARE ENOUGH FOR THAT OTHER PERSON TO WEEP FOR THEM. Love has compassion and concern for the other person.

Love is never:
hard or harsh
rough or tough
crude or rude.

If you love someone you want what is best for them. If speaking the truth in love is what is best for them—you do it! If keeping your mouth shut is what is best for them—you do that!

4. WATCH YOUR TIMING. When do you speak the truth in love? When a person is tired? You better not. When your husband has had a difficult day at the office or your wife has had a grueling day with small children at home? If you know what is good for you—you'll know that is not the time. Should you blurt it all out when the other person has a mass of oppressive problems that are weighing him down? That certainly is not the time to speak of anything controversial. What you want to do is find out where the other person is before you unload the truth in love. Take the time to listen and earn the right to speak the truth in love.

5. BE TACTFUL. Two people can say the same thing and yet get opposite results. What is the difference? It is *tact*. Often the difference in whether you use tact or not is determined by your voice tone. Sometimes it is by the words chosen or the way you arrange what it is you have to say. When speaking the truth in love it should always be preluded by something complimentary and said in a positive context.

Recently I was a guest on the Portland AM Show which is aired on Channel 6. This is one of those shows where they take telephone calls and I was to talk about one of my books. The lights all lit up and we had a great response of calls. After the show the phones were still ringing. So I answered some of the calls. Those that called were very complimentary as to what I had said on the show. Of course, I gobbled all of that up as if it were my favorite food!

One lady called and after saying some very nice things she concluded by pointing out a grammatical error that I had made and telling me that she was sharing this with me so that I could improve. Because her voice communicated love and she had been complimentary the entire conversation came through positive. I was able to accept this and to graciously thank her for her speaking the truth in love to me.

Later I thought about how hard it has been for me to receive any kind of criticism from other people but that my most outstanding growth as a person has come as a result of truth that was spoken in love by my best friends. IT TAKES A TRUE FRIEND TO SPEAK THE TRUTH IN LOVE.

WHAT A CHALLENGE IT IS—TO LEARN TO SPEAK AND TO RECEIVE THE TRUTH IN LOVE.

CHAPTER 12

Love Will Win The World!

"EVERYBODY HAS A DREAM,
EVERYBODY HAS A HURT,
EVERYBODY NEEDS TO BE LOVED!"
                              Robert H. Schuller

I am never happier than when I am with other people giving and receiving love. GOD'S KIND OF LOVE IS THE GREATEST—THE MOST FUN!

LOVE IS WHAT EVERYONE WANTS!

Stories about children have a way of staying in my heart long after I have forgotten other stories. The old story about little Johnny is one of my favorites. It was a cold Sunday in Chicago and Dwight L. Moody's Sunday School was operating as it did every Sunday. Arriving late in the morning was a little boy whose legs were blue from the bitter cold of the wind blowing across Lake Michigan. His coat was tattered and torn and pulled together at the top with a safety pin. Johnny had no hat on his head to keep him warm and wore worn-out shoes with holes in the bottoms without any socks. Taking the boy in her arms the Sunday School greeter began to massage the boy's half-frozen legs to stimulate the circulation. Then, sitting the boy down at arm's length, she asked him where he lived.

When the little boy told her, the lovable Sunday School greeter quickly calculated that the boy had walked more than two miles, one way, across the windy city of Chicago, on a bleak January morning, to attend the Sunday School of Dwight L. Moody. If any of you have ever been to Chicago on a January day, when the wind is coming in off Lake Michigan, you know how the cold can take away your breath!

"Why did you do it?" asked the friendly greeter. "There must have been a dozen churches that you walked past to come here. Why did you do it?" The little boy was a little shy and he hesitated a moment and then blurted out, "I guess, ma'am, it is because they love a fellow over here."

LOVE IS WHAT EVERYBODY WANTS! People will go to the ends of the earth to find love.

How do you win another person's affection and response?

> You cannot command it with words.
> You cannot force it or coerce it.
> It is love that melts the heart and brings people together.

You Can Win With Love!

BELIEVE ME—LOVE WILL WIN THE WORLD! There is a war being waged for the destiny of each man. Unlike other weapons that break and divide and destroy, God's weapon of love is the perfect one that heals, fulfills, and brings God and man back together. To every man who receives Jesus Christ, as personal Lord and Savior, God gives three things that make the Christian unconquerable in all his battles here on earth. They are: "FAITH, HOPE, AND LOVE—the greatest of these is LOVE." The word of God gives you the assurance that as you take up the weapon of love and use it in all of your battles you are going to be a winner. This promise is yours, "In all these things we are more than conquerors through Him that loved us." (Romans 8:37)

GOD HAS CHOSEN YOU AND GIVEN YOU HIS LOVE TO HELP WIN THE WORLD! The scripture is very plain that the way we love others is the sole sign that we have Jesus in our hearts. Make these great New Testament affirmations yours:

"Owe no man any thing, but to love one another . . . " (Romans 13:8)

". . . by love serve one another."
(Galatians 5:13)

". . . walk in love, as Christ also hath loved us."
(Ephesians 5:2)

"And the Lord make you to increase and abound in love one toward another, and toward all men, even as we do toward you."
(I Thessalonians 3:12)

HIS LOVE INCLUDES EVERYONE. A little boy asked me the other day, "How big is the love of God?" I said to him, "How big do you think the world is?" He put out each hand as far as he could reach and said, "It is bigger than big." I said, "Well, that's how big God's love is." Because the Bible says, "God so loved the world . . . " (John 3:16) God's love is bigger than our world. God's kind of love never excludes. It always reaches out to include. It is like a rubber band always stretching further. Love that excludes anyone or shuts them out for whatever reason is not God's kind of love. To call one's self a Christian and to be puny when it comes to love is to be phony.

REACH OUT AND TOUCH SOMEONE!

Never have I heard Otis Skilling's song, "Reach Out and Touch, "without being deeply motivated to love others more. Read some of the words:

"Reach out and touch the heart of
someone,
Someone who's lost his way;
Helping him find a new direction,
Showing him how to pray.
Reach out your hand of love."[1]

A so-called expert on Moses' law came to Jesus to
test his orthodoxy by asking Him this question:
"Teacher, what does a man need to do to live
forever in Heaven?" (Luke 10:25, TLB). Jesus told
him that the primary commandment was, "That you
must love the Lord your God with all your heart,
and with all your soul, and with all your strength,
and with all your mind." "And you must love your
neighbor just as much as you love yourself." (Luke
10:27, TLB).

"The man wanted to justify his lack of love for
some kinds of people, so he asked, 'Which
neighbor?'" (Luke 10:29, TLB). The man's question
was designed to evade the whole truth of love; to
get him off the hook, so to speak. So that he could
love who he thought was lovable and ignore
everyone who would not make his selection list.
Jesus seized the opportunity and told the story of
the Good Samaritan, to make it clear, that every
human being who is in need is our neighbor. No
matter if he is of our race or of another, lives on our
block, or on the other side of the world—he is our
neighbor. GOD'S KIND OF LOVE BREAKS
DOWN ALL BARRIERS—BE THEY REAL OR
UNREAL.

In the story that Jesus tells, we see that love is
more than just fancy words spoken in church.

165

1. From the musical *Love* (Kansas City, Missouri: Lillenas Publishing Co.,
© 1971). Used by permission.

Christian love responds to human needs wherever they be. No one is better equipped or more responsible to act and help persons who have needs than those who call themselves Christians. CHRISTIAN LOVE CAN NEVER BE PASSIVE. IF IT IS LOVE IT WILL ALWAYS BE MOVING INTO THE ACTION. You can't sit in the grandstand and claim to have His love. You have got to get out in the arena where people are bleeding and crying for what God has given you to give.

Ernest Gordon wrote a book entitled, *Meet Me At The Door.* In it he recalls the first time he ever met Martin Luther King in person. "The meeting took place at the old Trenton Station near Princeton where Gordon was Dean. The Dean took along an undergraduate student. As soon as the introductions were made the student asked Rev. King, 'Where is your bodyguard? After your attack of last year I didn't think you'd go anywhere without one.'

"Martin Luther King's face shown with a smile as he said, 'I don't need a bodyguard. I am in the Lord's hands, My time is His time. He knows what I have to do.' That morning in the chapel service, at Princeton, Martin Luther King spoke of the power of love and showed how it was God's kind of love that crossed the racial boundaries.

"After Martin Luther King was murdered Chaplain Gordon spoke to King's father. Just hours before the funeral Father King spoke of his son as 'M.L.' Lovingly, he told of how his son was such a gracious boy. He said, 'The devil would get into me, and I would give him a row. I would spank him. M.L. never said a word. He stood there with tears rolling down his face. He loved me. He never stopped loving me. He never stopped loving anyone. Why, I remember when he was but a little boy and we lived in the country. He met some families that had been thrown out of their shacks and M.L. came to see me at the meeting of the deacons. He told us about them so well that all my deacons were weeping. So, because of young M.L. the church took care of those families. We took them all into our houses. That was what M.L. was always doing, taking people in.' With tears flowing, Father King went on, 'I guess M.L. knew what would happen. He'd be late for a meeting because he had met someone. He was always late. I'd give him a telling off. He'd just smile. I know why he was always late. He had so much to do in so little time. He had only 38 years.' " [2]

WE MUST LOVE
WHILE IT IS YET DAY.
FOR THE NIGHT COMETH
WHEN OUR OPPORTUNITY TO LOVE
ON THIS EARTH
WILL BE GONE FOREVER.

A couple of months ago one of our fine young couples in our church had been plagued by erratic employment. They took it on the chin without complaints. Yet, their situation was becoming desperate. They needed help. One of our other young couples felt their plight and out of love

167

2. Ernest Gordon, *Meet Me At The Door* (New York: Harper and Row Publishers, 1969).

reached down deep into their own pocket and gave a love gift of $500.00. The couple who received the gift gave the glorious testimony that it was just the amount they needed to pay all of their bills. Can you imagine what this love response did for the faith and friendship of these two families? REACH OUT YOUR HAND IN LOVE!

Having just left the hospital, I was thinking about a friend who had a fatal disease when all of a sudden I was at a stop sign and had to bring my Mustang to an abrupt halt. As I looked to my left, in the middle of the sidewalk lay a woman screaming in desperation. I turned left and parked my car at the curb in front of her. On foot I hurried to where she lay. She was hysterical as she tossed on the sidewalk in the pouring rain. There I stood, trying to hold the hand of a strange woman who was screaming. I'm sure glad you didn't drive by and see me right then.

Finally, I got her to tell me why she was so frightened. This young woman had fallen and was eight months pregnant and was convinced that she had damaged her baby. With patience and steady assurance I was able to calm this mother and help her into the front seat of my car. There I prayed for her and for her baby. As I prayed she began to relax and became normal. By the time I had driven her the five or six blocks to her mother's home she seemed to be okay. YES, GOD'S KIND OF LOVE REPONDS TO HUMAN NEED.

The other night my seventy-one year old mother, who has been visiting with us from Ohio, was sharing with me some of the ways in which God has been using her life to minister to others. She has been going to a rest home in her town to visit and cheer the shut-in people there. A lady, Sally, was assigned to my mother to visit. Sally has a mental condition and had been abandoned by her husband in this rest home many miles from where he lives. For several visits Sally repeatedly told my mother that she didn't want to see her. She didn't want to see anyone.

Anyone who knows my mother very well knows that she has a great amount of determination, and she was not going to be that easily stopped from doing what she felt God wanted her to do. Mom talked to a sister of Sally and acquired the vital information that Sally liked bananas. So, the next time that my mother went to see Sally, she took a banana. A banana was like an ice cream sundae to Sally. She loved it.

In the weeks that followed, every time Mom went to see Sally, she took her a banana or some other fruit or goodie to eat. With each visit Sally began to respond. Soon Mother was putting her arm around Sally and giving her a little hug. Then, one day Mother was able to lead her new friend, Sally, into knowing Jesus personally.

Recently, at the close of a visit, my mother asked Sally if she loved Jesus. This forgotten woman, with a mental condition, answered, "I love Him a whole lot more since you've been coming to see me."

YES! LOVE WILL WIN THE WORLD!

LOVE IS THE *WINNINGEST* THING THERE IS IN THE WORLD! I HAVE SEEN IT:

MEND BROKEN HOMES

REBUILD BROKEN LIVES

CHANGE AN UNCONTROLLABLE BRAT INTO A LIKEABLE CHILD

TRANSFORM A REBELLIOUS TEENAGER INTO A RESPONSIBLE CITIZEN

BUILD BRIDGES ACROSS IMPOSSIBLE CHASMS

In a large city a woman was attending an evening meeting at her downtown church. Not giving it a second thought she left her car in a parking lot, under the care and supervision of the attendant, with the keys in it at his request. A couple of hours later, when she returned to pick up her car, it was nowhere to be found. The parking lot attendant didn't have the faintest idea what had happened to her missing automobile.

What would you say to a parking lot attendant, in whose care you left your automobile, if your car was then missing? Expecting a wave of accusations and big trouble, from the lady owner of the missing vehicle, the attendant became very defensive.

What happened next is unbelievable. There is no way to understand it but to simply realize that Jesus Christ was present in the life of this woman.

Presented with a panic-button-pressing happening she kept her cool. This Christian woman refused to react in any hateful or vindictive manner. With calm assurance she told the parking lot attendant that it was just an automobile and that she believed that God would take care of this problem. How true it is—the greater the crisis the greater the opportunity to really witness to God's love. The man was astounded. Never before had he seen such overcoming love in a live situation.

The next Sunday who should attend the lady's church? You guessed it, the parking lot attendant and his entire family. Better yet, they tell me that they have been there every Sunday since and now they are sitting close to the front!

A couple of weeks later the lady's expensive late-model car was found parked a few miles away with no damage whatsoever.

LOVE NEVER FAILS
LOVE ALWAYS WINS
BE A WINNER!

LOVE!!
LOVE!!
LOVE!!
NOT JUST ONCE
TWICE
THREE TIMES . .

BUT AGAIN AND AGAIN!

YOU CAN AND WILL WIN
WITH GOD'S KIND OF LOVE.

BELIEVE IT,
LOVE WILL WIN
THE WORLD!!